Cash In Your Diploma

By: Carl Schlotman IV

Cash in Your Diploma – Graduate with Your Dream Job

Carl Schlotman

Table of Contents

Introduction

My name is Carl Schlotman, and I was born and raised in Cincinnati, Ohio. I was recruited by colleges to play golf, after my St. Xavier High School golf team placed second in the Ohio State Championships. I chose to attend Queens University of Charlotte in Charlotte, North Carolina. I didn't exactly know what I "wanted to do" after college. Then, during my freshman year I met someone who used to be an investment banker, and after talking for a few minutes, I knew it was something I wanted to pursue. A Midwestern kid from a liberal arts school of fewer than two thousand undergraduates, raised in a middle-class family, I had no idea of the journey that stood in front of me. Not only did I want an investment banking internship, I set my sights on interning for some of the top investment banks in the world.

When I first decided on attaining the Goldman Sachs internship, I only had one alumni connection in New York to reach out to. I had to start the rest of my networking and internship hunt from scratch. I used an assortment of strategies and methods that I compiled for myself through trial and error throughout my college years.

This has been a pretty successful endeavor for me thus far. Since interning at Goldman Sachs, Brookwood Associates, TPG Sourcing Advisors, CapitalSouth Partners, and Merrill Lynch, I've had many students ask me for advice on how they might be able to achieve those kinds of internships too. They all wanted to know: how could a student from such a small liberal arts school compete against students from some of the best and most prestigious schools in the country – ones that even have classes to specialize in banking? I empathize with these students' concerns completely. There were several times during my journey that I wanted to just give up. Time and time again, I was laughed at, told that I should stop wasting my time, and ridiculed for not having the necessary pedigrees.

As I was walking into work at the 200 West Street building to start my summer internship, out came President Clinton. I had my Goldman Sachs badge on, and I was going to be there for the next three months. My dream of working on Wall Street had come true; I was one of the two percent of applicants who received an offer to intern with Goldman Sachs over the summer. Upon arriving at this illustrious financial firm, I quickly realized that my background was quite different from that of many of my fellow interns. I did not attend an Ivy League school, nor did I have the opportunity to go to a top-tier boarding school before college. I didn't grow up in New York City, nor do I come from a wealthy family.

I worked hard to get where I am, and I've been fortunate along the way. Now I want to give back from my experience and help you by providing the tools to unlock your full potential. I know your college years are supposed to be the best years of your life, and I certainly don't want to discourage you from thinking so. At the same time, I don't want to see you graduate and not be happy with your life because you have spent the last few years of your life not giving yourself the best chance for success. You attend college for four years of your life. Odds are that you will most likely work for more than forty years after graduation. I would hate to see you be unhappy for the majority of your life because you didn't take the simple steps early on. You owe it to yourself, your parents, and anyone that believes in you.

In this book I wanted to lay everything out that I learned in my process. I present to you the strategies that I used to attain such competitive internships and a job before graduating. I want to save students all the time that I undertook by trying and failing over and over. I want to help students get the internships they need to accelerate their career in their chosen field. The steps laid out in this book apply to everyone, regardless of their background. If the steps can work for a kid from a liberal arts school of only 2,000 students in Charlotte, NC, then it will work for you. Get started today on your path to earning the salary you want out of school, working in the field you choose, and role that most interests you.

Chapter 1

Establish Your Presence on Campus

From day one, it's important to establish yourself as a leader on campus. Making yourself known and establishing your credibility among your peers and professors will be very useful (as we will discuss later). This is advice you must have heard in other facets of your life: you need to figure out what you're passionate about and pursue it aggressively. For me, this was finance. I made sure I read the *Wall Street Journal* conscientiously. I read voraciously on the financial industry and I networked like crazy in the field. While you need to immerse yourself in your field, getting involved in clubs around your interest isn't necessarily the best use of your time. In my experience, you don't do much in the way of building a skill set, and employers rarely value involvement in clubs. Your time will be better spent allocated to outside learning, meeting experienced professionals, and reading material of your choice – all pursuits that can ultimately really help you get ahead.

Because you never get a second chance at a first impression, the way you dress is important. It may seem shallow or petty, but someone's first impression of you is based partly on your attire. I know it's tempting to think about wearing sweatpants and a T-shirt to class – but don't do it! At any given time you may run into someone absolutely unexpected, and you don't know what opportunities that might lead to. Whether it's a possible future girlfriend or boyfriend, or an alum visiting the campus who could possibly become your mentor, having the right attire optimizes the probability of success. Say your dream is to work on Capitol Hill, and your senator happens to be visiting your school for a lecture. When you see him walking down the hall, if you're wearing ratty old sweatpants and a T-shirt with holes in it, how likely are you to go introduce yourself? Your lack of attention to your attire might just negatively affect what could have turned into a major opportunity.

In my sophomore year in college I was with a group of people who wanted to go get some frozen yogurt after class. We made our way down to Yoforia, a frozen yogurt place right by school, an entrepreneurial start-up that had only a few stores nationwide, but was growing rapidly. When we walked in, a group of guys in suits were testing the frozen yogurt. Very unusual, I thought. One of the men seemed very familiar. When I'd first visited the store a few months earlier, it seemed a very unique idea, and I'd taken an interest in the company. I read a couple of articles about the CEO of the company, whom I also ran a search on, and found that he had purchased the frozen yogurt shop. The CEO had a fascinating background, and I'd always wanted to meet him. Well – there he was, one of the men standing by the frozen yogurt machines. I asked the person at the counter what the men were doing, and he replied, "The senior management from corporate, they are testing new flavors to build out our catering platform." This was my chance.

I walked over and introduced myself. "My name is Carl Schlotman. I apologize for walking up out of the blue, but I greatly admire what you've done in your career. Do you think I could pick your brain over lunch sometime in the next few weeks?" He replied warmly, "Absolutely Carl. I would really enjoy that, and thank you so much for coming up and introducing yourself." That day I wasn't wearing anything special, but nothing terrible either – just my normal khaki pants with a button-down shirt, with Sperry Top-Siders. I will never know if he would have been as receptive if I'd walked up in sweatpants, but I certainly felt like I was maximizing my potential for a successful encounter by dressing well. One of the morals of this story is that you never know who you might encounter on any given day, so be prepared to take advantage of the opportunities that come your way. Dressing the part is an easy way to be prepared. Of course, superficial appearances alone aren't enough. Another thing you really need to make sure of is that you treat the people around you properly.

The ability to be friendly and make good first impressions is crucial. Being a genuinely relatable person with a positive attitude will allow you to meet more people, and to have a better experience with every person you meet. Since satisfaction in life in large comes from the interactions and experiences we share with others, being a person that people want to interact with will not only enhance your college experience, but it will help with professional networking – and it will serve you all your life. A great exercise to practice this skill is the following:

When you're walking around on campus between classes, say hello to everyone you see walking past you. All you need to say is: "Hi, how're you doing?" And when they ask you in return, always say "Great." No matter what might be going on in your life, it's always a great day to be alive. This simple exercise will do three things for you. First, it will give you lots of practice and make you more outgoing and comfortable in reaching out to people. Second, you will be surprised at how quickly it brings a forth a smile from most of the people you encounter. Finally, I bet you'll find that this puts you in a more energetic mood. In the words of Ralph Waldo Emerson—"Always do what makes you uncomfortable." By being a more genuine person, you will not only have the chance to meet more people, but you will also have the opportunity to develop deeper relationships with the people you do meet. Each of those will contribute to your positive presence on campus.

At my first internship there was a business development employee named Bob. Every day Bob would make the rounds of the entire floor and say to each person individually, "Good morning. How are you this morning?" When the question was turned back on to him he replied, "I am superb." At first, I thought it was a little strange. Who on earth uses the word "superb" these days? Bob was showing his age... he sure wasn't a young whippersnapper anymore. But what do you think people thought of Bob around the office? Well, they simply loved him. The word *superb* brought a smile to almost everyone, and they naturally wore the smile after Bob's visit was over. And as you may guess, when Bob needed something done, he always had a loyal and supportive cast eager to help him. It's amazing how something so simple that only took fifteen minutes every morning had such profound results.

These are some things you should keep in mind as school begins, starting with the first few weeks, which are critical to establishing a presence on campus. Be the first to step up for icebreakers. I know this can be a daunting task, but everyone secretly respects the person that steps up boldly to be first. Once orientation is over, introduce yourself to the students around you that you haven't met yet. You never know who will become your best friends over the next four years. Shake hands and introduce yourself. (This is great practice for real-world experience, as well.) This is the fun part, even though you may not quite feel that yet. You may be nervous at first, and that is completely okay. Looking back on my experience, there were people that I was afraid to talk to, and they are now some of my best friends. Also, by stepping up first you'll get practice in delivering while nervous, and experience in leading when no one else wants to lead. Both are great skills to develop for the future.

Don't panic if you don't see the results right away. I remember many calls home communicating my worries that results weren't coming quickly. If the positive outcomes of all this aren't clear to you by the second semester, you'll surely see them when sophomore year rolls around.

CHAPTER 2

Goal Setting

"Setting goals is the first step in turning
the invisible into the visible."
—Tony Robbins

I learned the importance of goal setting as a senior in
high school, when I reached out to the most successful
businessman in Cincinnati, Ohio. He agreed to have
lunch with me (after I used several of the techniques for
reaching out to successful people, which I'll describe
later). Keith worked in insurance as his first job out of
school; he'd always liked the idea of working with
people and wanted to learn how to sell things. He really
enjoyed jobs where compensation was commission-
based because he felt like he was in control of his own

destiny that way. "The more I sold, the more money I made," was how he put it.

At a certain point, though, for the first time in Keith's career he thought he wasn't getting his fair share. He was the top salesman in the company and was not being valued as such. It was during this time that Keith took a trip to Las Vegas for a tradeshow. After a long day on the floor meeting with people, Keith sat down next to a guy at a bar. The man was an executive coach, and he initiated a conversation with Keith. Keith gets along with everyone, so to no one's surprise, they got to talking about a lot of things. Ultimately, the man asked Keith, "Have you ever thought about your goals?" Keith responded with, "Sure, I've always had a gross sales amount and a commission number in my mind, for every year." The man replied, "Interesting, but anything more long-term?" Keith fumbled this question as he searched for his response. He'd thought about his family and the goals he had for them. He had certainly at several points thought about the lifestyle he wanted, and maybe even the dream job he was after. But the answer to the man was "No." Keith had never actually thought about it in a careful, deliberate, planful manner. He came to the conclusion that he had really just made goals year to year, settling bets annually. Keith was ready for the man's sales pitch, because Keith knew that the man had found what he was looking for: a weakness to solve.

To Keith's surprise, the man asked him for a favor. "Do you think you could write down your one-year, ten-year, and twenty-year goals for me?" Keith said, "Sure, I appreciate the advice." On the elevator ride up to his room for that night Keith was definitely feeling curious, and he promised himself that he would do as the man asked. He was pretty busy over the next few days, which went by without any thoughts of his goals or the man at the bar. On the way home, though, 5,000 miles up in the sky, he picked up a napkin and a Delta pen. He started writing his goals on the napkin, and one of them was to "own my own company by the time I'm forty." That was a ten-year goal.

Flash forward to Keith's thirty-ninth birthday. After the celebration with family and friends, he went into the office and submitted his resignation. He felt that he knew manufacturing inside-out, and it was time to seriously tackle the goal of owning his own company. On that day after his thirty-ninth birthday, Keith was a business owner. He founded a company that would ultimately grant him the lifestyle and financial freedom that he was seeking. Who does he attribute the dramatic change to? He certainly gives the man at the bar some credit. "Goal setting is of the utmost importance. If you don't have goals, then how on earth do you know where you want to go in life? If you don't decide what you want, life will gladly decide for you. A dream remains a dream, until you write it down. That's when you've set a goal for yourself."

After hearing Keith's story, I wanted to make goal setting a habit. Much like Keith, I'd only set broad general goals that I never really tracked: make the varsity basketball team, play golf in college, get above a 3.5 GPA in school. For the next few months I researched goal setting by reading more than thirty books, ten academic papers, and any article I could find to use in determining my own goal setting system. I wanted a system that encouraged big-picture thinking to start, and allowed you to track your progress on a daily basis towards the big-picture goals.

I came across some very compelling information regarding goal setting. It seems that well over half of all Americans work at jobs that they never intended to do. They aren't passionate about their work, nor does it even interest them. Of course, these people tend to be unhappy with their careers. So how does this happen? How do people end up working in jobs they hate? A study by Dominican University shows that people who write down their goals and share them with a friend were 33 percent more successful at achieving their goals. If you don't determine what you want for yourself, the world will gladly determine it for you – as it has for more than 50 percent of Americans.

Step One: Start with the Ultimate Finish Line

You must create your personal goal setting system with the end result in mind.

Alice in Wonderland, being lost, asked, "Would you tell me where, please, where to go from here?" "That depends a good deal on where you want to get to," said the Cat. "I don't much care where," said Alice. "Then it doesn't much matter which way you go," said the Cat.

In order to make a road map you need to know where you want to go. Without thinking of the endpoint first, we could buckle down and work tirelessly, only to pick our heads up later and find out we aren't anywhere near where we want to be.

I have two recommendations for finding your life mission.

The first is to envision yourself on your deathbed. You are in the hospital, or maybe hospice has come to your home. Your life work is complete and you have only days left. Your wife, kids, siblings, colleagues, bosses, and friends have all been coming to visit you and say their good-byes. As each person comes up to your bed, what do you want him or her to say about you? Write down the response you would like to hear from each of your visitors.

Boiling down all the responses I had when I thought about this, these are the results I came up with: I wanted to have a positive impact on as many people's lives as possible; let as many people as possible have a positive impact on my life; and never stop learning. There you have it: that's my life mission in one sentence, and everything that follows will be an extension of that statement. You may be thinking about material desires, such as a Lamborghini or a beach house. That's okay; those are achievable too. Material goals are definitely an expression of human nature. I would love to own a Lamborghini just as much as the next person. At the same time, material possessions are not exactly what we're going for here. Have you ever heard of a midlife crisis? That occurs because people don't have a vision for the person they want to be in the long term – we're talking about character and values, the essence of a person. So they wake up one day as a person they never intended to be, and working in a field that never interested them. They try to compensate for this internal conflict by acquiring material possessions.

Step 2: Define Your 20-Year Goals

Why twenty years? Twenty years will put you in the range of 36-50 years old. At this age, we want to be living the dream. We want to have the job that the person we look up to now has, and say, "When I'm his/her age, I want to be doing exactly what he/she is doing." Twenty years from now we want to be living our own ideal lifestyle, with a comfortable financial situation, our family healthy and happy, and enjoying important life experiences.

To envision specific goals, you need to brainstorm all of the categories of your life that are important to you. For example:

1. Career (What industry, title, business ideas?)
2. Family situation (What does this look like, ideally?)
3. Financial status (What experiences do you want to be able to afford? Any material items that you would like to have? What salary or yearly income do you desire?)
4. Hobbies (Is there a certain handicap in golf that you'd like, do you want to play in a certain league, are there organizations that you want to increase your involvement in, or new experiences that you would like to have?)
5. Travel (What countries do you want to see? What activities are on your bucket list?)
6. Health (Are there certain things that you want to accomplish? Eating habits that you want to establish? A certain weight or physical condition that you want maintain?)

After you determine the answers, you must come up with concrete, tangible, measurable goals, so that you can hold yourself accountable.

Here's a selection of what other people have come up with, for their 20-year goals:

1. Be a managing director with a top 5 marketing firm or investment bank
2. Be a senior vice president within an organization
3. Own my own business
4. Be a CEO of a company
5. Have a salary of $100,000 or more
6. Have traveled to at least three new countries
7. Have met 15 people on my "mentors I aspire to meet" list
8. Publish my research in a top academic journal

Be as specific as possible. Always consider how you can quantify every goal when the time comes. You might set up an LLC around a grass-cutting business, for example. That would constitute owning your own business, but if it only generated $100 a month, would it be worthwhile – can you even live off of that?

Step 3: Make Your 5-Year Goals

Ideally, you're starting early with this, and Year 5 will be the year after you graduate from college. What do you want your life to look like after you graduate? The goals we're talking about should fall in line with our life mission and 20-year goals. For example, if your 20-year goal is to be a successful entrepreneur, then at least one of your 5-year goals should include:

1. Meeting a certain number of people who can help you achieve your goal
2. Building the skill set to accomplish the goal (e.g., in coding, finance, sales, or marketing)
3. Studying/interviewing people who have accomplished said goal (Mark Zuckerberg, Mark Cuban, Elon Musk, etc.)

Step 4: Break Your 5-Year Goals Down into 1-Year Goals

One-year goals should be similar to your 5-year goals, but smaller. For example:

5-year goal: read the autobiographies of fifty successful entrepreneurs. (I polled fifty CEOs and they read an average of ten books a year.)
Ideal 1-year goal: read the autobiographies of ten successful entrepreneurs.

Step 5: Create Daily Goals

This is my favorite step and it will provide the most frequent feedback and motivation. Use the tactics discussed above to deconstruct your annual goals into daily goals. By starting with the end in mind and funneling each goal down to the daily goals, I have found it possible to achieve goals I never thought would have been possible.

Annual goal: read ten autobiographies on successful
    entrepreneurs
Daily goal: read seven pages of a successful entrepre-
    neur's autobiography

There is a method behind the madness. Assume the average book is 250 pages. (Ten books with 250 pages each = 2,500 total pages; 2,500 pages/ 365 [number of days in the year]= 6.84 (or, in this case, 7: always round up to be safe). I recommend having a list of 10–12 daily goals that correlate with your ultimate 20-year goals categories. Once the daily list of goals is complete, enter them into an app called Lift (search Lift in the App store to download). This app is a wonderful tool to keep track of your progress. You simply input the goals in once, then check them off day by day as you execute them. The app keeps track of streaks and percent completion. If you have friends with similar goals, you can follow the same goal and even track each other. I'm a big fan of competition; it helps me focus and it's a great motivator. Technology changes rapidly, but right now Lift is my favorite to track goals.

Share your goals with five people you're closest with, even though some of the goals might be very personal.

I think you'll be surprised by how motivating this can be. The people you're sharing with need to be people who are willing to call you out when you're not keeping yourself on track. This is ideally a friend, parent, or sibling who rides you really hard. I know it can be annoying, but this will also allow them to channel that energy in a more positive atmosphere. Best of all, this will hold you much more accountable to achieving the goals you set out to accomplish.

Another way to hold yourself accountable is to print out the final sheet with your life mission statement, 20-year goals, 5-year goals, annual goals, and daily goals. Fold it up, and keep it in your wallet or purse. Whenever you get a few minutes of down time, take the list out of your wallet or purse and read through your goals. I do this frequently, for example, when I arrive to a class or a meeting early, and before bed. Another good habit is to write down your goals every morning and every night. I keep a legal pad next to my bed and I write down my annual goals and daily goals every night before I go to sleep and every morning as soon as I wake up. It may sound redundant, but it really focuses you on what's most important. It only takes five or ten minutes each time, and the payoff is tremendous. Taking this one step further, I even listed my goals on a poster board and hung it on my dorm room wall. (You might not want to display your goals so publicly on day one, though...) For me, it was really motivating knowing that if I came up short of my goals, everyone who had ever set foot in my room would know that I failed.

Notes to keep in mind when "goal-storming":

- Include everything at first, and edit later.
- Don't limit yourself. Often what seems like an overly ambitious goal is most achievable, e.g., writing a book, when you have never even received an A in English or literature. Ambitious goals are the most motivating.
- Make writing and reviewing your goals a ritual.

Most successful people are avid goal setters. They know what they want to accomplish and they go after it. Go to **www.cashinyourdiploma.com** to access a goal-tracking sheet like this.

Goal	Mon	Tues	Wed	Thurs	Friday	Sat	Sun
Wake up at 7am							
Write down goals morning and night							
Listen to audio book 1 hr a day							
Read WSJ							

CHAPTER 3

Campus Organizations to Get Involved In

First and second year students will find this chapter most useful. While seniors and graduates will also find helpful advice here, skipping this chapter would not cost you too much in the way of insight missed. Now that the disclaimer is over, here's the message: students tend to make a common mistake when it comes to deciding where to dedicate your time – the most valuable asset that you have. You can't buy time or create more of it. So you need to make sure that the campus organizations you get involved with are a valuable use of the limited time you have.

There are some organizations that match up with your hobbies, and I strongly encourage you to join those if time is available. However, this chapter discusses the organizations that will help us accomplish being a successful *graduate*. One of the first people on campus I recommend reaching out to is the alumni relations/alumni-giving department. It's their job to stay in contact with the alumni, get them to donate money, and make sure your school is thought of in a positive light in the minds of alumni. These people are responsible for most of the scholarship dollars that flow into your university. The alumni relations staff are usually very outgoing, confident in social settings, and great at meeting new people, in short, they're great to learn from in social settings. Their job depends on it. The alumni relations staff manages relationships with the elite donors. If you get a chance to attend an event with one of these people, make sure to do so. It is quite impressive. People who work in this function tend to be passionate about the school; frequently, they're even alumni themselves. They're great at meeting and engaging with people, and developing relationships. From there, they can sell the idea of the university and its future. This department has so much to accomplish and of course, there's never enough people or time in the day. This gives us the opportunity to help. The fact is, not many college students are keen on spending time talking with older people. Those students couldn't be more wrong in terms of strategizing for their futures. For those of us who see this for the opportunity that it most certainly is, here are ways to get involved:

1. Reach out to everyone in the department using the networking techniques I'll discuss later. Ask them to lunch. You will learn a lot from them about interpersonal relationships, and you'll be an asset to them, as well. Alumni love to meet current students and ask questions. You'll help the department meet their goal of giving alumni a positive experience.

2. Volunteer for the Student Alumni Council or any other organization similar to this. The Student Alumni Council (SAC) helps with any alumni events on campus, and represents the university in the surrounding community. Being a part of this specific group will give you direct access to your school's alums, allow you to observe and learn from those in alumni relations, and give back to the university you attend. At Queens University of Charlotte, SAC puts on an alumni weekend, a thank-you dinner for the top donors, and alumni reunions. These are the events that will give you the opportunity to access your school's most successful alumni, learn from them, and obtain advice from people that were once in your shoes.

3. Volunteer for a phone-a-thon or find a way to practice cold calling. The luxury of a phone-a-thon is that it's usually paid service, and there is no cost to you. I assure you, having to pick up the phone and call people you don't know will increase your communication skills, confidence, and character (at least after the first few attempts). I didn't have the chance to experience a phone-a-thon, but I practice cold calling through internships.

Many of you are probably thinking, "Why is it so important to meet alumni?" I'm sure you've heard the following from your parents: your job is to get good grades, so that you can get a good job out of school. Let me modify that purpose statement a bit. While good grades will help you get a good job, relationships play a bigger role than you think. Most alumni from your school are at a point in their careers where they can make new hire decisions, or at least have a say in the process. That is exactly the level of person that you need to be targeting. The best part about alumni is that you already have something in common; they're always willing to help because of that connection – and of course, they were in your position at some point in their life. Maybe they even had alumni help on their journey, you never know.

Another great organization to get involved in is a fraternity or sorority. Beyond committing yourself to a higher standard than the student who is not associated with Greek life, these organizations also add value in many other aspects. Much like alumni's desire to help a student of their alma mater, members of your Greek life organization can be an unbelievable resource. The wide reach of these organizations is astonishing. For, example Pi Kappa Phi has just under 120,000 members in several countries. The long list of alumni includes the founder of Red Box, Tommy Lasorda (Baseball Hall of Famer), and Roger Crouch (a NASA astronaut). Having gone to a small school, I utilized fraternity brothers to help make initial contacts. Brothers who had attended other schools and often on opposite sides of the country were more than willing to help me. Two of these men who started off as cold calls ended up being great mentors for me in my investment banking process.

I know this is not an uncommon experience. Many men and women have been introduced to opportunities that might not have been available if it weren't for these vast networks. Negative stigmas exist about Greek life, but I encourage you to look beyond the stereotype to see what these organizations offer. You may be pleasantly surprised.

Finally, I recommend any lecture series housed in your school. At Queens, we have the BB&T Leaders in Action Lecture Series. Hosted by the McColl School of Business, it brings in a high-profile business leader almost every month. The list of speakers includes: Alan McArtor (CEO of Airbus Americas), Ralph Ketner (Chairman and Co-founder of Food Lion), and David Singer (CEO of Lance Inc.). These speaking events on campus are beneficial in that they spark new thought, and help in career development and meeting new people.

Listening to the thought process and activities that leaders in respected industries engage in could cause you to see things in a different light. Most of the speakers are in the top 1% of their fields, and any insight you gain from their experiences could prove to be invaluable.

Their great advice and stories about their great experiences and lessons they've learned are not even the most valuable part of attending. Do people go to a talk by a successful speaker to hear their message and adjust their life accordingly? I think most do, but there is more to be gained from attending. If we do our homework properly we can find most of the information they'll speak about in newspaper articles, blogs, speeches on YouTube, or news interviews. Then why should we even attend? Already having the information and being prepared for the event allows you to focus your attention on key new additions and to ask a well-thought out and researched question in the Q&A portion after the speech. Asking a great question allows you to stand out from everyone else. It shows that you took the time to really care about the person and what they have to say. If well-executed, this will most definitely give you the opportunity to introduce yourself afterwards and follow-up on your question, and maybe make a valuable connection.

Before Alan McArtor, CEO of Airbus Americas, came to campus, I prepared by doing my typical research. I searched major news publications for any articles on Airbus over the last few years. I checked to see if Alan McArtor had made any comments in the MD&A (Management Discussion and Analysis) section of Airbus's financial filings. I then reviewed Airbus's financial performance over the last few years to understand how they're faring in comparison to their competitors; I made sure that I knew McArtor's background. That included where he went to school, and the path he took to get to the position he is in now. If you can find an autobiography on the upcoming speaker, that is the jackpot. What I found doing this homework was that Airbus had recently made huge strides in the United States. Under McArtor's leadership, they had taken market share from Boeing, their major competitor. Since he didn't mention that in his talk, I asked him, "I saw that Airbus Americas has gained market share as of recently over Boeing – what to you attribute the recent competitive advantage to?" I wasn't sure how I'd done, since he responded directly with a well put together answer describing strategies that differentiated Airbus. Afterward he was approached by quite a few people, and by the time I got to the front, he had a crowd of about twenty people around him. I thought my chance to introduce myself was impossible, but as I was walking up, he left the group he was talking to and walked towards me. He said, "You must follow the industry. Why the interest in aerospace?" After twenty minutes of talking about his background and the current trends in the industry, *he gave me his email address* to follow up for advice. The homework I did to get this advice and make this contact only took me, at most, forty minutes.

By getting involved with the right organizations and attending the best events, you will jumpstart your action plan to accomplish your goals. Get started today.

Summary

1. Get involved with alumni and alumni events.
2. Join in a phone-a-thon or some other way to get exposure to cold calling.
3. Look into Greek life at your school.
4. Take any opportunity to hear professionals speak on campus.

CHAPTER 4

The Infrastructure of You

When a contractor starts to build a house, he or she must first start with the foundation, and then the frame, which is necessary to support to future development of the house.

Just like the contractor, we to must build our infrastructure to support the process of attaining internships and/or jobs. It's a bit difficult to make this topic exciting, but it's vital for later strategies. The goal of this chapter is to equip you with everything you need to start your journey of attaining the internship/job you want.

The first critical item is your resume. A great resume is about the experiences that you have, and you especially have to focus on the formatting – it's key to have correct formatting. It shows your ability to produce good work and pay attention to detail. I learned this lesson the hard way. You have to present yourself well, because the whole point of a resume is to look so good so that you get people to invite you to a job interview.

After a thirty-minute taxi ride from LaGuardia, I arrived at the headquarters of one of the most elite investment banking boutiques. I was seated in a conference room full of fine mahogany furniture, and everyone there knew how big this opportunity was to their career. I was ready, or so I thought. I had spent at least three hours a day for the previous two weeks preparing for my big break. I was confident that there wouldn't be a single question they could trip me up on. The first interviewer came in and asked for my resume – no introduction or anything. He examined the paper and after a couple of minutes in silence, points out that in all the bullet-point sections, I don't have a period at the end of any sentences except for the one that he boldly circled in red. He asked if there was any particular reason that there was a period there. There wasn't a reason; I'd just accidentally added a period in there and didn't catch it. He automatically said, "If you can't pay attention to detail on your own resume, how can I expect you to pay attention to detail on your work for us?" And that was it. That was the end of my very quick trip to New York, and he led me to the front door. All of my preparation became irrelevant merely because I didn't have consistent formatting and showed a lack of attention to detail.

Resume

Lucky for you, I have provided a resume template compiled from many different successful resumes. Students who got internships with some of the world's most prestigious firms, including Wells Fargo, Ford, Siemens, Morgan Stanley, Coca-Cola, Microsoft, and Goldman Sachs. (Among others) The downloadable Word file can be found at **www.cashinyourdiploma.com**.

John S. Doe

Mobile: (704) 123-4567 • johnsdoe123@gmail.com
1900 Selwyn Ave. • Charlotte, NC 28274

EDUCATION

Queens University of Charlotte – McColl School of Business   **Charlotte, NC**
- Smith Scholar – Top 20% of Class   **Aug 2010 – May 2014**
- GPA: 3.85/4.0
- Major: Business Finance; Minor: Political Economy
- Alpha Kappa Phi Fraternity- *President, Treasurer*
- Men's Cricket Team

PROFESSIONAL EXPERIENCE

Scott, Fitzgerald & Co.   **New York, NY**
  Investment Banking Analyst   **June 2013 – Aug 2013**
- Authored the offering memorandum for a private equity firm's sale of one of it industrial services portfolio companies.
- Assisted in the development of the buyer's list, and participated in buyer calls.
- Prepared an LBO model identifying a prospective buyer's return over a five year investment horizon based on a wide range of entrance and exit multiples of EBITDA.

Marketing Associates   **San Francisco, CA**
  Marketing Summer Assistant   **March 2013 – May 2013**
  Assumed responsibilities for a $200 million skin care brand with 10% market share
- Analyzed Procter and Gamble's skincare communication strategy and presented a comprehensive plan to senior management focused on targeting psychographic sub-segments, which included an integrated media plan
- Conceptualized, edited, and approved artwork, coupons, packaging, instruction sheets, and displays
- Developed and assessed consumer research and product testing to identify product specific issues
- Reviewed sales by monitoring competitor's data, including forecasting 2014 and 2015 consumption and shipments.

Retailer Inc.   **New York, NY**
  Business Analyst   **Sept 2012 – January 2013**
- Evaluated financial performance of existing marketing vehicles to assist in the creation and implementation of a new marketing campaign, which included magazines, news media, updated website, and national press exposure.
- Created business development opportunities, including a loyalty program, merchandise program, and expansion models
- Managed client relationships, timelines, budgets, and expectations of top corporate clients inside of the services group

Atlanta Capital Advisors LLC   **Atlanta, GA**
  Summer Analyst Intern   **May 2012 – Aug 2012**
  $75mm acquisition of a an industrial manufacturer
- Ran leveraged buyout transaction models to provide valuation on prospective investment opportunities, evaluated appropriate capital structure, and reviewed multiple performance scenarios in order to manage return expectations
- Executed portfolio monitoring regimen on existing investments including: track and analyze portfolio companies' monthly financial results and covenant compliance, and forecast expected future financial results
- Authored key materials in support of the underwriting and portfolio management process, including: investment memoranda, executive summaries, and a 27 page internal research of aerospace industry trends

Fidelity Investments   **Denver, CO**
  Analyst Intern   **Jan 2012 – April 2012**
- Analyzed bonds, stocks, ETF's, mutual funds, and stock options to optimize ROIC for each portfolio
- Prepared models and analytical reports for clients to assist their determination of ideal risk allocation
- Compiled research and data to analyze trends of individual client's historical performance

Insurance Inc.   **Cincinnati, OH**
  Risk Analyst and Sales Support   **Aug 20010 – Aug 2011**
- Gained experience in sales and managing client relationships
- Provided sales support by preparing due diligence research, client information, and any other relevant documents

---

OTHER SKILLS / INTERESTS

- *Training the Street* Financial Accounting and Valuation Training
- Marketing Prep 2 Day Sales Boot Camp
- Highly skilled in Microsoft Excel, PowerPoint, and Word
- Proficient in Thompson Analytics, Sales Force, and Bloomberg
- Interested in traveling, playing golf, watching basketball, and reading

Cover Letter Email

Once the resume is done, you need an email address to reach out to contacts. You need a "cover letter email" to send with the resume. The template that follows works for cold emails, but can be adjusted for any given situation. The cover letter email is very important, because if it's ineffective and doesn't get the person's attention, they won't even look at the resume.

Subject: Introduction

Ms. Wells,

I am a junior at Queens University of Charlotte, and I am trying to attain a (summer investment banking internship for the summer of 2013). I have completed two internships in (Private equity: Edgewater Partners and TKP Advisors). I was wondering if I could get a few minutes on the phone with you to discuss possible (Investment banking opportunities with Wells Fargo). I have attached my resume for your viewing, and I look forward to hearing from you.

Sincerely,
Carl Schlotman

1. Specify the position that you are seeking and the time frame for which you would like to intern/work.
2. Highlight any past experience or school experience in your field of interest.
3. Restate your end goal.

If you don't get a reply, I would recommend following up approximately a week later, with some adjustments. On the follow-up email, I like to add my personal value proposition. This is different for each individual person and you need to come up with one of your own. My value proposition was: "I know I don't attend one of your target recruiting schools, but I am willing to do whatever it takes to work for you. I have gained as much relevant work experience as I possibly could to add value to you and your team." To come up with your own value proposition, ask yourself the following questions:

1. What makes you different from other candidates?
2. If you could only highlight one of your strengths, what would it be?
3. Why should this person listen to you?
4. What do you bring to the potential role that others might not?

There are many possibilities. Maybe you attend an Ivy League School and that's your strength. Or maybe you've attained an interesting perspective based on your unique background. Whatever it may be, you must be able to state it and then back it up. If you say you'll work harder than any of the other candidates they're considering, then you should have a very specific story or experience to back it up. (If you follow the effort level guide discussed later, you'll get a good sense of the tangible specifics to back up your claim.) At the end of the day, this one statement could make or break you.

Subject: Following Up

Ms. Wells,

I hope you are doing well. I just wanted to follow up on the email I sent you last week. (Paraphrase your personal value proposition.) I was wondering if I could get a few minutes on the phone with you to discuss possible investment banking opportunities with Wells Fargo. My resume is attached for your viewing, and I look forward to hearing from you.

Sincerely,
Carl Schlotman

If this follow up email doesn't work, you must develop the relationship further. Follow up can be done by sending relevant news articles to the person, asking to meet in person over coffee, company deadlines approaching, etc. You must find a reason to keep reaching out.

Create an Excel sheet to follow up with the people you reach out to. This will help you recall any previous interactions, as well as maintain the appropriate time between correspondences. This may seem unnecessary, but when you start to really get in the hang of the cold email and cold-calling strategies, you'll see it can get difficult to keep track of all your opportunities. My downloadable Excel sheet can be found at **www.cashinyourdiploma.com**.

Relationship Tracker

Cash in Your Diploma

Last Name	First Name	Date Contacted	Email Address	Title	Company	Facts Gathered	Next Steps	Last Contacted
Smith	Sandy	3/22/2013	Smith@ marketing.com	VP of Human Resources	R&R Marketing	Went to Princeton, played tennis, is traveling to Tampa Florida next week, the internship deadline is April 3, 2013	3-Apr	2/19/2013

LinkedIn Account

You *must* have a LinkedIn account – it's the Facebook for professionals. LinkedIn is very useful in tracking relationships, finding potential prospects, and doing your homework.

Step 1:   Go to **www.linkedin.com** and sign up. Create a profile. The set-up process is very intuitive and should only take about twenty minutes.

Step 2: Upload a professional-looking picture of yourself. I recommend that you wear what would be required of you in your field (e.g., a suit for most industries or scrubs for medical professions). Statistics show that adding a profile picture to your account makes it seven times more likely that someone will click through to view your profile.

Step 3: Copy your experiences from your resume into your LinkedIn profile.

Step 4: Invite all of your family, friends, and professors to link with you. This is a great way to start expanding your network.

Step 5: Networking allows you to see who your close contacts know. If there's anyone who could be professionally useful, for an internship or any job, you can ask your contact for an introduction.

Aside from your Excel sheet of contacts that you'll develop in your networking, LinkedIn is a great way to track who you meet through the years. Overall, LinkedIn is about quality, not quantity. I only connect with people that I have an active, current relationship with.

Clean Up Other Social Media

We all have a personal brand. Everything we post on the Internet helps define it. Employers, future business partners, and associates will view these networks. If something is on there that you would not like them to see, take it down. Invest an hour and go through your social media. If you are under twenty-one, don't have any pictures of yourself drinking alcohol. A good rule of thumb is, if you wouldn't want your boss, parents, or grandparents to see any particular photo or post, take it down. Also, check your privacy settings. Regardless of what content is on your Facebook page, it doesn't need to be viewable by strangers. I recommend reading *Brand Aid* by Larry Linne and Patrick Sitkins for more on this topic specifically. As more and more channels to share information are available to us, it's becoming essential to manage the brand that you want for yourself.

Interview Attire

Dress to impress. What you wear to an interview is of more importance than you might think. According to Princeton psychologists Janine Willis and Alexander Todorov, a first impression is made in just one-tenth of a second. That gives the interviewer barely enough time to judge your appearance. One-tenth of a second doesn't even get you to a formal handshake. If our first impression will be based on appearance, let's make sure we make the most of it.

I highly recommend business suits for men and women both. Traditional colors of black or navy blue tend to yield the highest success rate. Women often ask, "Skirt or pants?" I would recommend pants – you won't have to worry about appropriate length or seating position.

Search online for forums that will discuss interview attire for your specific field. The best source of advice on interview attire will come from those currently in your field.

Interview Preparation

Make sure that you give yourself the best opportunity for success. In the words of coach John Wooden, "Failing to prepare is preparing to fail." The whole idea of being resigned to "you are who you are" and "letting the cards fall as they may" is just an excuse to put in less effort. It's necessary to do our homework! While I'm framing this in terms of a company interview, it applies to freelance and graduate school interviews as well. There are two questions that I've been asked in every single interview I ever had. The first one is: Tell me about yourself. You need to have a well-polished answer at the ready. Below is an example of a great response.

"Absolutely. I was born and raised in San Diego, California. I started swimming at a very young age and it has always been strong interest of mine. After placing first in the state for the 100 fly, I was recruited by several different schools. Also from an early age, I had a mentor who was a financial advisor. So thinking about finance has been a part of my life for a long time, and I always knew I wanted to consider finance as a profession. I chose NYU because of the opportunity to continue swimming and to be close to finance in the city. After my first internship at an investment banking boutique I knew it was something I wanted to continue doing. I've worked on smaller deals in the middle market, and now I want to get experience with larger deals. That's why I'm here today."

The second question you must be able to answer is "Walk me through your resume." Know what's on your resume and as you expand on the bullet points listed, make sure to move in chronological order, and give the interviewer the opportunity to dig deeper after you finish. You can close with something like: "If you'd like me to expand on any of the points further, I'd be more than happy to do so."

Company Interview Preparation

Prepare detailed due diligence on the prospective company. You should know the company's history (including when and where they were founded and by whom). Know if they are public or private. If it's a public company, know the ticker symbol, the two-to-four letter combination the company trades by on the public markets. You should definitely be aware of who the senior people in the organization are, and what positions they hold. Find what products or services the company provides, its key customers, any competitive advantage, and what they pride themselves on. For example, Southwest Airlines promotes itself as the low-cost airline. That is how they differentiate themselves and the pride in their company. They also get a lot of positive press on their unique culture. If the company or university you're considering is said to have a unique culture (and most of them think they do), dig deeper to find out what that actually entails. If you are able to speak on that, it would show you are proactive, and highly interested in them, which is always a plus. This may sound basic, but always carefully review a company's website prior to interviewing. Also, try to read any of the materials they have put out, whether they're marketing materials, their annual report, or something else. This could give you insight into how they format and structure their final work product. It also might tip you off on possible interview questions that might get thrown your way – or bring up questions that you'd like to ask them.

Technical Questions

These are more common in finance and any other highly analytical jobs such as consulting, programming, and research. This is your chance to shine, and you need to make sure you give yourself to the best shot to do so.

Research any guides published for your industry, such as the Vault guide or any case study interview guide for consulting. If you can find a guide on your topic, invest in yourself and purchase the material. Not only will it benefit you for your interview, it will make you a better intern once you start. Also, check any online forums for questions that are common for your industry. An example would be to search things like: "Most common interview questions for computer programming online." Start with those questions and try to find more. There are also forums that former candidates and interns will post questions they were asked or interview prep material that was helpful to them. (**www.Glassdoor.com** is one example)

Previous Interns or Employees

Reach out to former interns or employees of the firm you're interviewing for. They might be able to shine some light on interview questions they were asked, or talk about any preparation material they received while they were with the firm. Obviously, they're also a great resource for learning more about the firm and its culture. It is also a great way to build your network, since you know have the prospective firm in common. Depending on how open your contact is, you may even ask for advice on the other points discussed above. Some firms expect different interview attire and preparation than others. Any intelligence you can gather from former interns will be very beneficial to your goal.

Lay the groundwork for your future success. These steps and processes are absolutely necessary foundations for everything you'll do subsequently. Not applying the concepts in this chapter would be like building your dream house on a sinkhole. Don't cheat yourself here; if you do, you'll pay the price down the road.

Summary

1. Resume – and pay attention to details!
2. Get a LinkedIn account.
3. Manage your personal brand.
4. Invest in your interview attire.
5. Do your homework to succeed.

CHAPTER 5

Importance of Building Relationships

Networking has always been important to success in business, and it's even more essential for the millennial generation. Our parents, most of whom are baby boomers or from Generation Y, had career maps with different drivers. They went to work for large corporations such as Procter & Gamble, Ford Motor Company, and Bank of America. They worked hard, got promoted, and with a promotion came a raise in salary. The company gave them job security in exchange for their loyalty.

However, for our generation the environment is much different. There is very little external job security. If you're not the best match for the position at any point, or if no longer bring a skill set that adds value, then you can easily and quickly be replaced, or your job may simply be eliminated. You don't think so? Well, neither did the employees of Lehman Brothers. Analysts making anywhere from $80,000 to $150,000 a year were instantly out of a job upon Lehman's collapse. With advanced technology, increased global competition, and suboptimal economic environments affecting more and more jobs in the marketplace, can we obtain job security? The answer lies in the relationships you form. I learned this very valuable lesson from someone on my personal board of directors. He invited me for dinner at his house, and as we sat down, I inquired about a person he introduced me to a few months earlier.

John, the person I was asking about, was a senior account representative for a company that was a top supplier to the financial industry. My dinner host told me that John had just been laid off, as of a few hours ago. What a way to start dinner! For some reason, though, my mentor didn't seem to have the same reaction as I did. He said, "John will have something by the end of the week. There is no doubt in my mind that he will be just fine." How on earth could someone be so certain in such a turbulent economic climate? It turns out he was right — because he knew John religiously followed the rule that he was about to teach me.

He continued, "I've observed over the past seven years that there's a lot more to John, which you may not have been able to completely comprehend in four hours with him on the golf course." John had climbed the corporate ladder quickly, and he covered the top two clients of his current firm. John hadn't attended an Ivy League school, and he was completely new to Charlotte area upon moving his family here. But this is what's most critical: John understood the importance of relationships. He always made the extra effort to get to know his clients, colleagues, and the same for people he was meeting for the first time. Of course John had always added value to his clients and that is certainly of utmost importance, but then again, he'd been fired in the recent layoff of 10,000 people. It was the large web of relationships that John had amassed over the last several years that would save him. He understood that relationships really do matter. The good news for John was that this understanding of relationships allowed him to land a new and even more senior position with a similar organization, within days.

Summary

1. Job security is partially reliant on the people you have genuinely connected with and to whom you have added value.
2. The value of strong relationships is priceless.
3. You don't have control over economic cycles, but you do have control over finding ways to add value to contacts, clients, or superiors.
4. There is always space and money for people who add value.

CHAPTER 6

How Good Relationships Become Good

I was excited: I'd met someone on my "people I aspire to meet" list. It may sound strange, but yes, I do have such a list. On it are thought leaders, esteemed senior executives, cutting-edge entrepreneurs, and extraordinary athletes, and each one is someone I've studied or someone whose work I read, someone I'd love to learn more from. This man I'd just met had been on my list since I started college. He was twenty-six and had a budding career in finance working for some of the best advisory firms the country, and most recently had founded his own company and was the CEO. I'd heard his name many times from people in finance, and everyone admired him. Brad seemed to know everyone, and there was always such a positive reaction when his name came up.

"I finally met Brad," I said to my dad. But my dad wasn't sure what to make of that; he didn't know of Brad. I quickly gave him Brad's bio and described how I had wanted to meet him for quite some time. Dad replied, "Well, how was it?" I said, "He invited me to another event next Friday." My dad responded with, "That's awesome. Did you learn anything from meeting him tonight?" The question puzzled me — what could I learn just from introducing myself? I said, "I introduced myself and got invited to another event!" It was my dad's turn to be puzzled, and he responded, "I thought since you look up to him, you might have observed him and learned something about what contributed to his early success. But it sounds like you might have another opportunity on Friday?" Trying to understand, I asked, "How can I learn how someone has been successful, while we're at a networking event with cocktails?" Dad's answer was clear. "If you look up to him, there must be something you can learn from him. Watch him closely, and I'm sure he'll reveal something about how he's gotten to where he is today." He had a good point, and with that I was excited for my opportunity on Friday.

I showed up at the appointed time, with two goals in mind. The first, to meet new people, and the second, to observe Brad to see if I could pick up on anything that may have attributed to his success. Hours later, I called my dad. "I did what you said! And all I came up with is that he smiled a lot and he doesn't do much talking in the conversation. That isn't very helpful!" There was a pause. I had him! Dad replied, "Well, are you are you sure there isn't some significance behind both of those behaviors?"

Well, yes, after all, my dad was right. I have found that people who are successful smile often. And it's inevitable that people want to be around folks with positive energy. A smile is often contagious and naturally puts you in a better mood. "When you say that Brad didn't talk much in the conversation, do you have an idea why that was?" I answered, "He was just genuinely interested in the other person and what they had to say." I had learned two very valuable lessons.

Once you start to expand the list of people you're able to meet, keep track of them and what you learned from them using the template in Chapter 4. Another way to do this is by connecting with them on LinkedIn.

As I thought about this lesson, I actually realized that I had first been exposed to it when I was in high school. I was selling discount cards for a local restaurant as a fundraiser for my summer baseball team. I traveled door-to-door around the neighborhood trying to sell as many cards as I could, and I soon realized that another local high school was selling the exact same cards – the entire high school was selling them, not just one sports team. There were about 100 kids selling the same cards to only about 300 houses. I almost felt bad every time I approached a door because the first comment every time was something like, "Another person is selling those darn cards!" My goal was to sell ten. I had sold nine and was just looking to get the one remaining card out to someone. My last stop was going to be at a man's house just around the corner. He had a young son who loved sports, and could usually be found playing in the front yard. As usual, I stopped for a few minutes to play catch while he hit baseballs off the batting tee. Then I headed to his door to sell his dad my last ticket.

The boy's father answered and immediately said, "Not interested. I've had twenty kids come to my door, and I just don't have the cash. Don't you kids know what it's like out there?" I didn't know what to say, and I walked away after he closed the door. I was shocked. I had hit close to one hundred houses by then, and had never just plain failed that hard. I was disappointed. I sat on the corner for a few minutes thinking about what just happened. All I could conclude is that I needed to sell one more ticket, so I proceeded on. I tried twenty-five more houses with no luck. After a full two hours of knocking on doors I hadn't sold that magic tenth ticket.

It was about time for dinner, so I headed home and I wasn't too happy. My mother told me in an uncertain voice that Mr. Jones wanted me to call him. I was terrified – that was the man who had just scolded me a half hour earlier. "Hello, Mr. Jones. This is Carl Schlotman, my mom said to call you back?" Mr. Jones said, "I would like to buy a ticket." I was shocked. That was literally the last thing I was expecting. What I *was* expecting was round two of the explosion that had occurred earlier. In my astonishment, all I could do was mutter, "Thank you." My parents were also very surprised that Mr. Jones decided to buy a ticket – apparently Mr. Jones had been laid off a few months back and couldn't find another job. I'd heard about the effects of the 2008 crash in the news and read about it in the *Wall Street Journal*. But this was the first time I actually really appreciated the effects myself. About two years later when Mr. Jones and I were simultaneously raking leaves and I walked over and asked him about the experience. "What changed your mind about that restaurant ticket?" It took a while for him to recall. "It was a really hard time for me and my family. We truly didn't have the cash to do it. But when my kid came in and asked me why you were the only big kid that ever stopped to play with him, I had to buy one from you."

This idea of genuinely caring about other people has completely changed my life. I love getting to know new people and learning about what's important to them and how I can be of assistance. I've learned so much through getting to know the different people I've had the opportunity to meet over the past few years. We have so many different backgrounds, worldviews, skills sets, and expertise, and it's always fascinating to me to meet someone new and learn how he or she thinks, and see things from their point of view. I can't stress this enough: if it weren't for being genuinely interested in other people, I would not have been afforded the opportunities I've had. Embracing the people around you opens doors that would otherwise be closed.

Being genuinely interested in others will not only help you build relationships, but it will also make you a more attractive person to connect with at events. People like to be around positive and interesting people. When you can connect common experiences and interests that you share with someone, chances are that you will deepen that connection.

Of course (and as I've said before), the best way to learn these concepts is to practice. Nothing can substitute for experience. Find some events or environments where you can practice these ideas. Even try them out at the next party you go to. President Bill Clinton is well-known to have practiced his social skills during parties at Oxford.

Everything in this world – including each one of us – exists in relationship to something else, and what creates happiness is shared experiences with others. Whether it's common childhood experiences, sports moments, obstacles overcome, shared hobbies, or same travel destinations, connections with others enhance our lives. It's a shame that the word "networking" has a negative connotation in some circles, driven by people who pride themselves on the *number* of LinkedIn connections and business cards they have, or the number of famous people they know. This person can be found at conferences or events handing business cards to *everyone,* talking about themselves, and how "you should be a client." It is a true shame, because in my experiences these people have it all wrong. Their success is superficial, and thus, not sustainable. With the right approach, the value of real, personal networking is infinite.

Smiling Challenge: The next time you walk to class, make sure to smile all the way. Observe your general mood during and after the exercise. Observe how your smile effects the facial expressions of those you see in passing. Don't be surprised at the number of people that smile back. And if this works anything like it did for me, you will feel like a million bucks!

Lessons

1. Make it a habit to smile as much you can.
2. Be **genuinely** interested in others' interests, needs, and importance.
3. Keep track of the people you meet along the way.

Chapter 7

The Art of Inspiring Dialogue

It's through dialogue that trades and skills have been passed down from generation to generation throughout history. Since I was young, my parents always encouraged me to talk with people who were smarter than I was, more experienced, and had more money. So I engaged with people in my neighborhood that seemed to be doing really well for themselves. There is something transcendent that comes with getting advice from someone who has been incredibly successful, someone with years of experience and wisdom, and often in a field completely different from mine. Just a few months ago, I had the opportunity to talk with one of the world's top multiple myeloma researchers for over an hour. It was an amazing experience to be able to pick this scientist's brain, and to learn from their advice and deep experience. Dialogue is how we learn.

So, one might ask, what is the art of inspiring dialogue, and where does it take place? You've heard of the informational interview. (I don't like to use that terminology, as these conversations often develop into much more than information being shared.) Inspirational dialogue is the act of seeking advice from experienced and knowledgeable professionals that will share their path, advice, and assistance with you. Everyone has something to offer. Everyone has the ability to teach you something that you don't know. The beautiful thing is that people love to teach. People inherently want to help others. Every single person had a unique upbringing, with different life experiences that mold and shape the way they view problems or situations. The art of inspiring dialogue allows you to view things differently from the way you usually do. It gives you access to another point of view and a method of thinking though things. If you choose to view the world understanding that everyone has something to offer or teach you, I think you will be very surprised and gratified. You'll be more well-rounded, and equipped with different ways of viewing the complex problems we face in today's society.

Why should you partake in inspiring dialogue with others?

If you are able to embrace the mental framework discussed above, the sky's the limit as far as what you might learn from other people. Anyone can be a resource for you, and maybe even help you solve any current issues you're faced with.

1. Inspiring dialogue can give you a window into many different careers in a short period of time. If you're considering a broad category such as technology, reaching out to people can help. Say you've narrowed it down a bit, to the following careers after school: hardware technology, software technology, at either a start-up or a more well-established technology company. Instead of trying to complete internships in all these places, reach out to people you can talk with who know about each of these areas. In a thirty-minute conversation, you can typically rule out – or rule in – some of the options you were considering pursuing.

2. Reaching out to people in your field is a really superb way to get career advice. It can be so beneficial to get advice from someone who was once in your shoes, and has since become successful doing what you aspire to do.

3. You can establish long-lasting and beneficial contacts. If the person you're networking with isn't able to help you in an immediate fashion, often they will offer to introduce you to someone else who can help you. If they don't offer that during your conversation, then politely make the request. "Thank you again for taking the time to talk with me. Do you know anyone else who might be good for me to meet? I'd really like the opportunity to have a similar conversation with any helpful person you might suggest."

4. The worst scenario is that you now have a connection with one more person who knows you and what you're trying to accomplish – and that's not too bad after all, is it? If they hear of opportunities that could be of interest to you, or if they think of anyone it might be helpful for you to know, they will often reach out to you. If you don't reach out and engage in inspiring dialogue, you definitely won't get introductions for the opportunities you are seeking.

Who should I try to talk to?

You want to talk with the most experienced and knowledgeable people that you possibly can. Read up in your field to find out who's doing big things and who have been large influencers in the past. Ideally, these are people that you aspire to meet and look up to. They might even be people that you read about in class assignments. Some of the best conversations I've ever had were with the people I studied or people whose work I read. This allows me to ask much more detailed and interesting questions. If you think that someday you'd like to be doing what this prospective person is doing, then reach out.

How do I reach out to these people?

I usually either meet people for coffee if they are anywhere within 45 minutes of me, or I set up a phone call with them. Below is the email I typically use to reach out to people that I'd like to talk with:

Dear Chris,

I hope you are doing well. I am a college student at Queens University of Charlotte interested in finance. I've seen your name on several occasions in connection with your terrific work, and really admire what you have been able to accomplish. I'd really appreciate the opportunity to seek advice from you over coffee or a phone call. Thank you so much, and I look forward to hearing from you.

Sincerely,
Carl Schlotman

That email should do the trick. Tracking your correspondence is a good idea. If the person you're writing to is in a very senior position, then expect to reach out multiple times before you hear anything back. I typically like to wait a week from the time I sent an email before I follow up with another very similar email. It isn't that the individual in question doesn't want to meet with you, so don't take any lack of response personally. Most of the time, they just have a lengthy to do-list, and you aren't among the top few items. One of the CEOs I interviewed for this book said, "Don't be afraid to follow up. I lay out a to-do list of about ten or fifteen items that I need to get through every day. Sometimes some items don't make the list. It doesn't mean that I don't want to get them done. It just isn't of the utmost importance at the moment. I don't view the emails following up as nagging, by any means. I really appreciate the follow up, and if anything it shows persistence and interest – both traits I admire."

Where can I find great people to reach out to?

First, check out these lists online: the Forbes 30 Under 30, Inc.'s 5,000 List of Fastest Growing Companies, Fast Company's Most Creative People, and others (including local lists). The easiest way to get started is by searching top (insert your prospective career here) in (insert your location or where you would like to live). For example:

Search top graphic designers in Houston, Texas. You can pull lists from the Internet, and look at the other ways that will yield an even higher return rate.

1. As we discussed earlier, take advantage of the speakers who come to your class or your school. I'm always amazed by the number of students who just walk right out after a guest speaker gives a lecture on a topic of interest to them. This is an opportunity given to you on a silver platter! Usually when people are willing to come to speak to a college class, they have some additional motive to be there. Often they're looking to mentor students from their alma matter, trying to give back because someone did so for them, or they might be looking for interns or job candidates. Make sure to always introduce yourself to the speaker. First of all, it's courteous to thank someone for taking the time out of their day to come talk to your class. Second — you never know what may come of it. If you're armed with an intelligent question about the lecture they just gave, you might find yourself accepting a paid internship doing exactly what you want to be doing. This happened with one of the students I was helping just two weeks ago. Rami wanted to get into public relations, and especially social media. Anyone interested

in this space knows that it's difficult to find a position doing this work, and extremely hard to get a paid opportunity, without prior experience. Rami (a second-semester senior) and I met for coffee on a Monday to talk about his future. I walked through some of the ideas in this book, and particularly this idea about engaging with visiting experts. Two days later, a woman came in to speak in one of his communication classes. She owns her own non-profit whose mission is to draw attention to and subsequently, funding for philanthropic causes. Rami found her talk interesting and approached her after the class. They met for coffee the next day, and the upshot was – he had a paid internship. Rami's now doing public relations and social media, making $11 an hour instead of working for free. This is the result of taking the extra step of five minutes to talk with the speaker.

2. Seek to participate in your school's alumni events. Alumni like to meet and talk with current students, and this is a great place to ask for a more in-detail meeting with the alumni that you really want to connect with. (Review chapter three for the information on how to get involved.)

3. If you have any professors who had really interesting careers before teaching, sit down with them during

office hours, or meet for coffee. Professors can be a wealth of knowledge and contacts. I had a professor who'd been the CEO of a publicly traded textile company in North Carolina — I actually had one-on-one access with someone who'd had to fight a takeover battle against Carl Icahn. (For non-finance people, Carl Icahn is one of the wealthiest activist investors of all time.) College provides rare opportunities for you to have access to such people.

Here is a check-list to make sure you are looking at all the options available to you.

Networking Outreach Checklist

Cash in Your Diploma

Source	Additional Notes	Completed
Immediate Family	Mom, Dad, Brother Sister, Grandparents	
Extended Family	Uncle, Aunt, Cousins, Second Cousins	
Family Friends	Ask the first two groups if they know anyone that can help you	
Alumni	High school alumni, alumni of your college, sports team alumni, academic associations	
Fraternity/Sorority	Alumni of your organization or older members	
Alumni Advancement Office	Access to the Database of Alumni (or Career Center)	

Personal Friends	From sports, clubs, schools, associations, social events	
Personal Friends Parents	Maybe the above group has family that can help you	
Volunteer Groups	Any philanthropy activites you have been involved in	
Neighboorhood Friends	The people that live around you	
Speakers	Anyone that you have heard speak or has come to your class	
Professors/ teachers/faculty	Ask your professors for introduction	
Social Networks	Linked In, Facebook, Twitter, Instagram	
Religious Affiliations	fellow members of the same religious institution	
Networking Events	People you have met at events	
Co-Workers	Anyone at your previous or current job that can help you	
Military	If you were active military any connection from that experience	
Politicians	Especially the ones that represent you (They tend to know a lot of people)	
Email	Search your inbox for anyone that you may have forgotten	
Doctor or Dentist	Make sure to let them know what you are tring to do - Their networks are very broad	
Hobbies	Golf, tennis, basketball, chess, video game groups- Common Interest	
Airplanes	Introduce yourself to the people sitting next to you (You never know)	
Google Search	This is your last resort as it will have the lowest success rate	

You can download the actual excel file at

www.cashinyourdiploma.com

The most common mistake made when people are trying to expand their circle of influence is that they don't cast a big enough net. There are people available to them just one or two connections away, and they don't know. The key is to make sure you take advantage of the connections you already have made, and make sure you reach out to as many people as possible.

What are good questions to ask?

You must do your homework, as we discussed earlier! I always gather detailed background on their past work experience and anything else they're involved in. Read anything they've written or had written about them. This does two things for you: it allows you to ask more intelligent, insightful, and in-depth questions, and second, it shows that you are interested, and that you care. Some of you might worry and wonder if it's a little creepy. Well, that question has come up frequently, and my response is, "I like to inquire about the people I aspire to meet in hopes that it will make our conversation more valuable." The response has never been negative. Most people find it flattering that you took the time to learn about their background. I know I sure would. Here are a few questions that I recommend asking (and where necessary, substitute terminology that belongs to the field you're interested in):

1. I saw that you went to Princeton and studied economics. Did you know you wanted to go into investment banking at that time? (Inquire about something that you found in your research. It shows that your interest is sincere.)

2. When you were first getting into the business, why did you decide to work for Wells Fargo over other banks?

3. What are the skills or characteristics you possess that have allowed you to rise to such high levels in your industry?

4. When you think of the people that have worked for you in the past, what makes a great analyst? (If "analyst" isn't appropriate, insert the proper job function.)

5. If I am interested in getting into investment banking, what can I be doing now to prepare myself to succeed?

6. Are there any books or resources that were instrumental in your development that you could recommend for me?

7. What are three pieces of advice that you would give a college student such as myself?

For the very introverted people out there, you can read biographies or books on the thought leaders in your field. This isn't as beneficial because it isn't personal advice specifically for you, but you will still gain insight. My best advice for you here, is to tough it out and conquer your bashfulness. It could be a whole new beginning for you, and it would be so worthwhile.

Aim high! The possibilities are endless. If there's a Forbes 30 Under 30 list (or something like it) in your area, reach out to them. It doesn't matter if they're CEOs or head political honchos, you'll never know if you don't ask. The worst any of these people can say to you is no. You have nothing to lose, right? How do you think I met Keith (back in chapter two)? You bet, it was by using the strategies in this chapter. You have everything to gain, and the upside is limitless.

CHAPTER 8

Internships are the New B.A.

"When I was a 21-year-old intern at CBS, I was told I had crossed eyes and shouldn't try to be on air. That's when I decided I was going to be behind the scenes."
—Andy Cohen

"My biggest bit of advice would be to spend some time actually helping caterers or chefs, even if it has to be for free or as an intern of culinary externship. It helps immerse yourself in what you potentially want to do."
—Giada De Laurentiis

"I started in the mailroom, literally, as an intern... in 1974. The legislator I was working for at the time said, 'I want you to get your law degree and come back here and get elected and be the first woman governor.' I kind of took that guy seriously - I thought that sounded like a pretty good idea."

—Claire McCaskill

"I think the lie we've told people in the marketplace is that a degree gets you a job. A degree doesn't get you a job. What gets you a job is the ability to carry yourself into that room and shake a hand and look someone in the eye and have people skills. These are the things that cause people to become successful."

—Dave Ramsey

Apprenticeships have always had their place; they're how the human race has passed down skills, knowledge, and crafts from generation to generation. Benjamin Franklin only had two years of formal education. His father was a soap maker, and it was customary in that time to learn the business of your father. Franklin hated the soap business, but had developed a strong interest in books. His father took him around to several skilled workers in town to find him an apprenticeship. They settled on an apprenticeship with his brother James.

He learned to write and edit under his master, and it was through this opportunity that Benjamin Franklin was able to purchase his first few books. Many of the seeds of thought and innovation that occurred during his apprenticeship would later help him blossom into the innovator, entrepreneur, and esteemed politician we hold in such high regard hundreds of years later. But apprenticeships are not only a tradition of the past. Think of some of the most successful and talented people of the last few decades. How did Oprah Winfrey, Steve Jobs, Steven Spielberg, Conan O'Brien, Tom Hanks, or Betsey Johnson make the list? Have you ever thought about how each one of those successful people rose to the top of their given field? Well, they all share at least one thing in common. They all started as interns. At one point in time, each one of those people was at the lowest level of the food chain.

Oprah Winfrey: We know her for being the host of the highest rated talk show ever. Oprah is also a generous philanthropist. She started as an intern for WLAC-TV, the CBS affiliate in Nashville, Tennessee. After performing well as an intern, they hired her full-time to deliver the news.

Steve Jobs: In high school Steve Jobs cold-called William Hewlett, the co-founder and president of Hewlett Packard.

Steve was hoping for some parts he needed to do a school project. Packard gave him the parts he needed and offered him a summer internship. It was during that summer internship that Steve Jobs met Steve Wozniak. (And the rest is history!)

Steven Spielberg: A three-time Oscar Winner, and two-time director of the year, Spielberg landed an unofficial internship with Universal Studios when he was seventeen. He did not have access to the studio; so every day he woke up early to sneak in.

Tom Hanks: Nominated for an Oscars five times, Hanks won two of them for being best actor. Before he "made it," he interned for the Great Lakes Theatre Festival in northern Ohio. Now he's one of the best actors of all time.

Betsey Johnson: She's one of the most innovative minds in fashion, and she got started by interning for *Mademoiselle* magazine.

Students can no longer afford to coast through four years in college, get a degree, and count on getting a job. The marketplace has changed because of technology, globalization, and economic circumstances. Students who study media and communication are seeing the technological changes occur right in front of their eyes. They learn marketing strategies using direct mail, radio, and even television, only to see the target customer demographic shifting to social media like Facebook, Twitter, and Instagram. It's impossible for textbooks to keep up with our rapidly changing environment (and that's one of the reasons that even textbooks are going digital!). The hardware that we're learning on is changing rapidly, as well, so that it's becoming more and more difficult for schools to purchase state of the art technology as well.

So how are employers who are looking to hire these students after school responding to such changing environments? Executive Director of the Cincinnati Film Commission, Kristen Erwin, says, "We are looking for relevant work experience. I get thousands of emails from young aspiring entertainment graduates wanting to work in different roles for each movie. The diploma from a good school is checking the box. We will only consider students with substantial work experience." Companies want you to be equipped with a skill set that will bring value to their organizations. If you are at all interested in public relations or marketing, Gary Vaynerchuk's books are must-reads. You are not competing against the person next to you, sitting in the same room as you, or even in the same school as you. You are competing against young students across the United States, India, China, and every other country in the world. The power of the Internet no longer requires you to be in the same physical location. We are globally interconnected, and that has absolutely increased the competition. And we don't have the power to control economic cycles. Students must prepare for the worst, and we happen to be recovering from the worst economic recession since the Great Depression. It's definitely time to get serious.

You're probably asking, "How on earth do I get started if everyone is looking for prior work experience?" This is exactly why you need to get started now. There's no time in your life that you'll have more flexibility than you do today. You don't have a mortgage to worry about, spouses or children that you're responsible for, and all the other responsibilities that come with growing older. You know what it's like to have no money, and you aren't all that opposed to sleeping on a couch if you have to. This makes your opportunities endless. You have the ability to work for some of the brightest leaders in your field, because you can offer to work *for free*. I worked at one of my most transformational internship experiences for free. I so badly wanted to get into the investment banking and private equity arena, but my only option to compete against MBAs was to work for free. Offering to work for free says a lot about a young person's character and passion for the job.

Charlie Hoehn is a great example of leveraging unpaid work into big things. Charlie graduated from

Colorado State University in 2008, right in the middle of the great recession. He spent twelve weeks trying to find a job – almost every company he applied to turned him down. The few offers he did receive were for very low pay and not at all what he wanted to do. He aspired to do work he *wanted* to do. The strategy he came up with was to work for free. He found people he wanted to emulate and reached out to them via cold emails. He offered them free advice on ways to improve their website and free video editing. He started working for authors like Seth Godin, Tim Ferriss, and Tucker Max. Months later, he got a full time job offer from Tim Ferriss. Charlie has now published several books and is doing the work he wants to do.

The numbers don't lie. Look at these stats:

"The 2012 Internship and Co-op Survey and the Student Survey Class of 2012 revealed that 63% of paid interns received at least one job offer upon graduation. In contrast, only 36% of graduates who have no internship experience received at least one job offer."

Go do whatever you need to do to get into the field that interests you. I did two unpaid internships before I got paid to do the same work. Sure, those internships were hard. I was working a lot and money was really tight. But I ended up making $15,000 for two and a half months of interning the summer of my junior year. If I hadn't done the unpaid internships I wouldn't have had that opportunity. The money evens itself out over time.

Lessons

1. A Bachelors degree alone doesn't get it done.
2. Be the next leader in your field by getting the internship you want.
3. Remember that everyone has to start somewhere.

CHAPTER 9

Diploma Education v. Outside Education

I feel like I've had two educations during my college years, both necessary for learning and growth. Unfortunately, more importance is placed on one over the other. My first education is one that most people participate and believe whole-heartedly in: my formal education with Queens University of Charlotte. It's important to learn how to learn, to execute time management, and to understand the foundational theories essential to your field. For medical students, science students, and computer science majors, this education is exceedingly important. For the rest of us,

I would argue that the informal education a person can receive outside the classroom is just as important, if not *more* important. There are four main ways to gather this informal education outside of the classroom: internships, personal learning material, online classes, and successful people. The best part is that most of these learning outlets are completely free, and one of them can even pay you money to learn.

Internships

Internships are one of the only ways to roll up your sleeves and get first-hand experience in what you're interested in doing after graduation. There is no better way to find out what career path interests you than getting an internship, where you see, hands on, what the job is like every day. Interning also builds a strong network. When you're able to produce great work and add value during the internship, you build a list of people who are known evangelists for your ability. There is something new to learn every day during an internship, and overall, I'd have to say that internships are one of the most effective ways to develop during college. I wouldn't have done six of them if I didn't feel so strongly about their benefits.

Personal Learning Material

I strongly advise any college student to read for at least thirty minutes a day. It's extremely important to pick up material relevant to your career aspirations in newspapers, books, interview preparation material, magazines, blogs, or podcasts. For finance, I read any books or articles recommended to me: finance books that make bestseller lists, the *Economist*, Vault guides, the *Wall Street Journal*, the *Financial Times*, and certain blogs. To find the material relevant to you, do some Google searching. If you can identify the leaders in your field, look for interviews with them, and articles by or about them. If you can't find anything there, ask them! Here's a sample script:

> Secretary: Hello, this is the office of
> (your target contact)
> You: Hi, this is Carl Schlotman calling for (your
> target contact)
> Secretary: May I ask why you are calling?
> You: Absolutely. This may seem a little out of the
> ordinary, but I'm a young college student, and I've
> followed (target contact)'s career for quite some
> time now. I finally built up the courage to call for
> one piece of advice. Do you think you might be
> able to help me in any way?

That usually does the trick. Be specific as possible when you get the person you are trying to reach on the phone.

Online Classes

I have taken several online classes in my collegiate career, many of them (by choice) to gain a deeper understanding of my major, and to take more challenging classes than those that might be offered at school. I've also taken courses in topics that I knew literally nothing about, but was curious about learning more – ranging from clean energy to computer programming. These websites are taking the education world by storm. The student has the ability to take the class whenever he or she feels like taking it. These online platforms provide courses taught by some of the best professors in the world in their strongest subject. The best part is that it is free of charge. The platforms that I recommend are:

1. Coursera.org
2. edX.org
3. Khan Academy

Learn From Successful People

1. Reach out to the people you admire in your community for informal interviews for you to learn more about their career path, as discussed. Email them or call them and ask them if they would take a few minutes to meet for coffee.
2. The Academy of Achievement maintains a treasure trove of many great interviews with elite thinkers in

business, science, public service, art, and sports. This resource is completely free and gives you access to the minds of some of the most talented people to walk this earth.

3. Read five to ten autobiographies on the top people in your field. This is also a great way to prepare for making the call later. I've successfully done this with several authors I admire.

4. Email them asking whatever you're curious about. This can be a good strategy with senior people who are extremely busy and might not have time for a phone call. Of course, calling them is best, but this should definitely be used as a back up to calling, as it can be very effective. Below is a copy of the email I sent to Gary Kelly (CEO of Southwest Airlines); you can use it as a template for your own letter.

Dear Mr. Kelly,

I am a current student at Queen's University of Charlotte. I have followed your career for quite some time now, and I really admire what you have been able to accomplish as the CEO of Southwest Airlines. What would be a few pieces of advice that you might have for a young college student like myself?

Sincerely,
Carl Schlotman

Just a few of the people I've gotten advice from include Gary Kelly (CEO of Southwest Airlines), Dave Dillon (CEO of Kroger), George Buckley (CEO of 3M), Michael Carpenter (CEO of Ally Bank), and Fred Smith (CEO and founder of FedEx). If by any small chance any of the men above are reading this book, *thank you so much.* I think it's amazing that people of such stature would take the time to write back to a kid, and it speaks a lot to the character of these leaders and their organizations. It's no coincidence that many of the companies listed above were used as case studies during my undergraduate college career. I thought that getting personal advice from the people I was studying in business school was a very neat way to supplement my formal education. Here's advice from these incredible leaders:

Gary Kelly- Follow the Golden Rule, make each day count, and stay true to your values.

David Dillon- Develop a natural curiosity about any topic you take in school. Becoming a lifelong learner will help you grow every year. Seek out opportunities to practice leadership even while in school. Encourage your friends, peers, and family to give you constant feedback on how you are doing as a leader and friend. Book recommendation: *7 Habits of Highly Effective People.*

George Buckley- Read history on the lives and ideas of great men and women. Start with George Marshall, Horatio Nelson, William Wilberforce, and Benjamin Franklin. Don't go to college for fun. Go there to get the best education you can extract.

Fred Smith- Become technically competent in business. Find a business you enjoy and at which you can excel. Read Peter Drucker, Ted Leavitt, Henri Fayol. Also read the biographies of General George Marshall, as well as Thomas Watson, and other business executives.

Get started supplementing your formal education. The opportunities available to you are endless. There are incredible people out there willing to give advice. You just need to take action.

Lessons

1. Read material beyond the required reading for class.
2. Take online classes in specific areas that you want to learn more about.
3. Seek advice from people in roles that you hope to potentially attain in the future.

CHAPTER 10

The Telephone is a Deadly Weapon

"Life is way too short to be small."
—Benjamin Disraeli

Audacity is a game changer. Chances are that any great achiever you look at has made one audacious move at some point in life. For example, Gary Cohn, COO and president of Goldman Sachs, is in charge of the operations of one of the largest financial institutions in the world and makes well over five million dollars a year. One might guess that Gary probably attended an Ivy League school, got recruited on campus because he was brilliant, and could recite by heart the hundreds of textbooks he read on finance.

However, on digging further, you'd find that it was Gary's ability to be audacious that landed him a trading job with one of the top firms on Wall Street.

Here's an excerpt from Gary Cohn's commencement speech at American University:

> I went through what I consider to be the formality of trying to go out and seek a career and seek a job. I ended up luckily landing a job with a division of United States Steel in Cleveland. Not a job that I had any aspirations for, not a job that I really wanted, but I had to appease my father and I had to go out and get a job. The only good news is that I was at that job from July first to Thanksgiving my graduation year. By Thanksgiving I had found a way into the financial markets, by pure drive and perseverance. I'll tell you a little story about how I got my first job in the financial services industry.
>
> As I said, I was working for the United States Steel in their home products division. I was in Long Island for the week working with one of the sales offices. I made sure that I worked very hard Monday through Thursday and got all of my work done and convinced the gentleman that

I was working for that I had never been to New York City and I wanted to go see the city and could I leave early on Friday. He agreed to that. I literally took myself to the Commodities Exchange Center which at that point was in Four World Trade Center, went into the Commodities Exchange Center...found my way up to the visitors' gallery and realized that everyone in the visitors' gallery was just like me, trying to figure out what was going on there. I figured out that if I go down one floor, I'm actually down at the trading floors. I got down to the trading floors and I don't know what I thought I was going to do. I stood at the security entrance to the trading floors and stood there for about three or four hours, trying to figure out what to say to someone...trying to figure out how to get a job and trying to figure how to introduce myself.

About four o'clock, I literally gave up. I walked to the elevator bank. I dejectedly hit the down button to go down to get a taxicab to go to the airport to come back. And, I hear a gentleman say, "I got to run, I'm going to the airport." I jump in the elevator with him and say, "I overhead that you are going to the airport." He said, "Yes, I am." I said, "What airport are you going to?" "LaGuardia." I said, "Do you mind if I share a taxi with you?" He said, "Sure, by all means." I didn't know him and he didn't know me. I thought, "Well, here's my shot. I've got 45 minutes, in traffic on a Friday afternoon to convince this guy that I'm hirable and need a job." He literally went through and grilled me on my knowledge of financial markets, grilled me on my knowledge of certain aspects and I think I moderately passed. By the end of the taxi ride, he says, "What do you know about options?" I said, "Everything." He said, "Great, I want you to come back Monday, I want you to interview. I'm trading options, it's a brand new market that's opening and I don't know how to trade it and I need someone to stand behind me and tell me exactly what to do." I said, "No problem, I'm your guy." I literally got home Friday night and my first stop on the way from the airport was the bookstore. I bought the McMillan *Options as a Strategic Investment* book and read it four times—as I said, this dyslexic guy read it four times over the course of the weekend and came back in and interviewed and was offered a job. That's how I started in the financial services industry."

Amazon's Jeff Bezos received his undergraduate degree from Princeton University. After graduation, he pursued a career in the intersection of computer science and finance. He worked for a New York City firm that was helping brokerage firms to clear trades. From that job he moved into quantitative hedge fund trading, and got some experience in a business model where computer programmers program computers to make trades. That was when Mr. Bezos really started to understand the unbelievable potential growth in the Internet. He left a great job on Wall Street with this crazy idea to sell books on the new thing called the Internet, something that no one was doing at the time. If it weren't for that moment of audacity, we wouldn't have the ability to buy goods online through Amazon.

Obviously, we can think of many ways that audacity can play to our disadvantage. Any extreme acts that could tarnish our brand image or reputation would be detrimental to achieving our goals. So in this chapter I'm going to talk about the strategies we can use to harness the power of audacity.

Our millennial generation has come into contact with so many different methods of communication in our lifetime: we've all used text messaging, Facebook chat, email, Instagram, Snapchat, Twitter, and lots more. These are all great tools, and have greatly increased our connection to friends and family. Think over the last few communication efforts you made. When was the last time you actually called someone on the phone? Chances are that if you actually called someone in the past few days, it was a family member, significant other, or one of your closest friends. Can you recall the last time you called a friend that you don't interact with regularly? It seems as though our generation is only comfortable calling close contacts because over the phone everything is live. There isn't the time to think and reply, or ponder and craft a response, or the ability to put off a difficult conversation once you answer the phone. But that is exactly how we will use it as a wonderful tool to get you what you want! That device invented long before Twitter and Facebook has worked wonders for me, and it will work wonders for you, too.

College students looking for internships or jobs out of school are often told, "Apply everywhere!" Most claim that the more applications you fill out the greater your chances of finding something. While I'm a very big believer in hard work, and the notion that more action yields more results, unfortunately, that does not apply here. Applications do not work. Let me repeat: don't bother applying online through company websites to get internships. The only time it's acceptable to do so is if an employee currently with the company asks you to do so. Inboxes that receive these resumes are a type of black hole. They are screened by computers for keywords to narrow down the number of applicants because it isn't often feasible for the human resources team to read through every single resume they receive. If you want to take these casino-like odds, then be my guest and just keep applying online. In trying to find my first few internships, I meandered around and probably filled out over 500 applications to corporate internships. The fruits of my labor resulted in zero interviews. I was very frustrated by the end of it. I knew I needed to find another way, and I rethought my entire perspective. The most frustrating part was that the process felt so inhumane. Not once in all these applications did I get to talk with someone directly. How could I get a foot in the door if I couldn't even talk to anyone? That's when I moved to cold-calling. Cold-calling sounds bold and it may make you nervous just to hear those words . . . it certainly made me nervous, but I was ready. I had Mr. Johnson, a vice president at a local private equity firm, all lined up. In front of me in bold blue font were his phone number, address, and email. I then proceeded to sit there for the next three days finding everything possible to help me procrastinate and avoid calling Mr. Johnson. I was stuck, and just couldn't bring myself to make the call. I called one of my mentors in Charlotte, and asked him what he thought of me cold calling prospective internships.

He said, "I think that's a great idea, Carl. Have you made any calls?" I answered him, "That's where I'm struggling right now. I can't seem to find the courage to make the call." My mentor's response: "Hmm. Well, do you have an internship or a relationship with this firm now?" Obviously my answer was no to both of those questions. My mentor: "What's the worst outcome if he says no to your call?" My reply: "I don't get an internship with his firm." My mentor: "Carl, I don't see where you have anything to lose."

With that call, I learned a very important lesson that would play out multiple times in my college journey. When you have very little to lose, there is much more upside potential than vice versa. I made the first call, and after an awkward couple of minutes, Mr. Johnson shot me down. I should have been disappointed, but it was a neat experience. I wanted to get better at calling for internships. I knew I had many improvements to make to my script. I made it my goal to do at least twenty calls a day for the next two months. I wanted to find a script that would yield a success rate of higher that 50 percent (success defined as setting up an interview) and here it is:

Carl: Hi, this is Carl Schlotman. How are you doing this morning?

Prospect: I am doing well. How can I help you?

Carl: I do realize I'm calling you out of the blue, so I'll be brief. I'm currently a junior in college and I want to get into investment banking. I know I don't attend one of your target schools, but I promise you that I'll be a better analyst than any of the other kids you might be talking to. Do you think you could put me through an interview?

Prospect: I'm in the middle of something right now. Sorry, man.

Carl: I completely understand. I am sure you are a very busy woman/man. Do you think we could set up fifteen minutes to interview this Wednesday?

Prospect: Wednesday doesn't look good for me. Sorry

Carl: That's okay. How does Thursday or Friday look for a brief fifteen-minute call?

Prospect: I am just really busy this week.

Carl: I promise this won't be a waste of your time. All I am asking for is an opportunity. It will only take fifteen minutes of your time.

Prospect: All right, call me at four o'clock on Thursday.

Carl: Perfect. In the meantime could I send you my resume?

Prospect: Sure.

Carl: What's the best email for you?

Prospect: <u>John@crg.com</u>

Response: Thank you so much for the opportunity and your time. I look forward to talking to you Thursday.

Simple, right?

Now, here are some more potential objections that you might encounter:

Prospect: I'm sorry. I just can't help you.

Rebuttal: I understand that you have much more important things on your to-do list. What can I do to convince you that I'll be a great intern for you?

Block: Well, Carl, we just don't recruit from your school.

Response: Just give me a shot; ask me any technical question you can think of. Can I come into the office [if local] this afternoon or do a phone interview [if long distance]?

The goal of any cold call is to obtain an interview. It's extremely difficult to get the internship or job without getting an opportunity to show the firm what you can do. I found that the script above had an 87 percent success rate of getting an interview, based on the sampling of two hundred calls I made. That rate was much better than the five percent success rate I had on my first twenty-five calls using other cold calling scripts. Just as I learned along the way and made adjustments, so will you. There is no script or plan that makes it entirely unblemished through battle. But it is great to have a guide with you.

Now that we have an idea of what you're going to say once you get these people on the phone, we can discuss how to get their contact information. There are six good strategies. I have ordered them from most effective to least effective.

1. Warm the cold call: Reach out to people in your network who know the person you're trying to get in touch with. A very good resource for this is LinkedIn, and it's why it's so important that you set up an account (as we discussed in the chapter on the Infrastructure of You). LinkedIn will allow you to see if you have any mutual contacts with a specific person. If so, you have the ability reach out and ask if they could either make an introduction, or if you might be able to reach out

to your target contact and mention their name. This would look like the following:

You: Hi, Mr. (or Ms.) (so and so). My name is (blank). How are you?

Prospect: Doing well.

You: (Insert contact's name) recommended that I reach out to you. I am really interested in getting into (insert profession) and I would really like to talk with you about your experiences. Or any opportunities that you may have at (insert firm name).

2. The prospect is much more likely to talk with you, given the mutual friend. Be very considerate when planning to use this strategy. You MUST ask the mutual friend if you can use their name. *Under no circumstances is it okay to use their name if they have not given you the okay to do so.*

3. Enlarge your pipeline of potential contacts. At the end of your interview or phone call, always ask if there is anyone else in the office that it would be beneficial to talk with. Try to get more than one name. If you do this effectively, you will only need one break at each firm before you are off to the races.

4. Rapportive: This is a great application you must add to your Gmail account. With it, you can search possible email accounts for the person you want to contact; all available contact information will show up on the right-hand side of your screen upon entering the right email.

5. Company websites: Many smaller firms list management's contact information on their website, along with their respective bios. Always check for this, as it's also a great place to gather intelligence on the company. If they ask where you got their contact information, be honest and say from the website. Most people will really respect the effort.

6. Company documents and PowerPoint slide presentations are often available online. More times than not, they will have a couple of slides at the end with the contact information for those who gave the presentation.

7. Find the office building number online and start from the bottom, literally. I used this strategy for many of the banks. I'd call the lobby, and ask for someone within the organization. This is a bit of a difficult path, as there are most likely at least three secretaries to get through. Once you are relayed past the front desk, ask the secretary for her number in case you're disconnected.

At almost every place I've worked, there's one secretary working for, on average, six people. So once you've got the secretary's number, that is a central opportunity to six potential contacts. If you don't know the names of the people this secretary works for, the following script usually does the trick:

You: Good (morning /afternoon). My name is (insert your name), and I'm very interested in getting into (insert profession) I'm a college student and I am new to all of this. I hope you can be of assistance: I'm looking for one specific piece of advice. It will only take two minutes of (blank's) time. Is there any way you can possibly help me?

Secretary: (Pause) Here you go, good luck.

The phone will beep and you will be relayed to someone.

Now, there are much better days and times to call on people than others. I would strongly recommend avoiding Mondays. Typically people are busy with meetings and dealing with anything that may have come in over the weekend. I've found the best days to call are Tuesday, Thursday, and Friday, with Tuesday and

Friday having the highest rates of success. I found the best times to be from seven to nine a.m., and then at the end of the day, from five to eight p.m. EST. These are the best because you can usually bypass secretaries, and there is a slower workflow for anyone who's there at that time. This makes it much easier for someone to take a few minutes to talk with you.

These times also vary from industry to industry. For investment banking, I had the highest success rate from eight p.m. to eleven p.m. It is best to research your given field and ask mentors that are currently working in your field to find times that will be best for you to call.

Be audacious – go get what you want. And always try to stay positive when executing the ideas in this chapter. When it comes to making calls, it's all about persistence and confidence. Make twenty calls using the strategies in this book, and odds are you will have to suit up for at least a few interviews this week. Go hit the phones.

CHAPTER 11

Securing the Right Internship

Many students ultimately get internships. But then they work with the firm and leave the experience feeling as if those last few months were a waste. (If you've had one of these internships, you completely understand.) This chapter will help you avoid those internship programs.

First and foremost, you must know what you want from your internship experience. If you don't know what you want, the firm will decide for you, and you may end up answering phones at the front desk more often than if you'd set your sights higher. You simply will not leave the experience as satisfied. There are many takeaways that you can seek from an internship experience, including: connections, skills, training, senior level exposure, mentorship, or testing to see if you like the profession. All of those end goals are perfectly acceptable, but you need to decide what you want before you start. This is essential, because it can allow you to help design the internship to be mutually beneficial for both parties. Here are some examples:

Insurance: I wanted to learn how to sell, especially because I thought this was an essential skill in anything you choose to do career-wise. So my supervisor and I structured a plan that gave me as much access to insurance agents as I wanted, and I even called on prospects myself.

Private equity: I wanted to build a skill set, learn modeling, practical valuation application, how to structure deals, introduction to debt, and mentorship from one of the best in my geographical area. I got exposure to several live deals, mentors who were incredibly talented, I observed the process of buying a company, and all the modeling behind debt return for investors. Through this experience I learned that this area was absolutely fascinating to me, and was most of the reason that I chose to do leveraged finance at Wells Fargo upon graduation.

Investment banking: Many of my mentors and people I aspire to meet started in investment banking. I wanted to gain the perspective of working in between senior level executives and interested buyers. It is also fascinating to get exposure to many different industries and how companies make money. Also, the experience in dealing with different financing needs of companies is very interesting.

Figure out what you want from your internship so that it adds value to your path. As we've discussed – you can't devise a clear path to getting to your goal, if you don't know where your goal is.

I have always reached out to at least ten prior interns for each of my internships, for several reasons. I want to know what they thought of their experience. They have no reason not to be truthful, and they're ready to provide an accurate view of the job with no sugarcoating. This can help you determine whether the internship you're considering will meet the goals you want to achieve in your experience. Also, take note of what the former interns are doing now. Most internships tend to exit their interns intern into specific positions for full time work after school. For example, investment banking internships tend to move their candidates into full-time investment banking programs or into private equity. Keep track of what firm the former interns are working for, and in what position. Ideally, the firm's former interns are either still with the firm or they're working for some of the best companies in their field. If it's a good match, chances are that being an intern at the prospective firm will be a positive step for you.

Just make sure that you've thought about whether the prospective internship is in a field or job that you want to work in after college. A large percentage of students that intern get full-time offers after they graduate. So, you can see that it's important to align your internship experiences with what you want to pursue after school.

If you don't have access to former interns, then ask the people that you're in contact with about the internship. Ask them some of the following questions to gather intelligence on the role:

1. What skill sets will I develop through interning for you?
2. What are your former interns doing now?
3. Who will I be working with primarily?

Lessons

1. Is this internship in a field I want to be in after graduation?
2. What skill sets will I develop as a result of this internship?
3. Is there a potential mentor that I'll work closely with?
4. Have I reached out to former interns to gather intelligence?

CHAPTER 12

Cowards Quit-Effort Levels

"Never make excuses. Your friends don't need
them and your foes won't believe them."
—John Wooden

"Finding your purpose may be a lifelong pursuit,
or you may have discovered it when you were
five years old. There's no absolute timeline for
anyone. That's a good reason never to give up,
to keep on discovering things every day."
—Donald Trump

I want to start with the story of Viktor Frankl, the author of *Man's Search for Meaning*, which has certainly had a lasting effect on my life. Separated from his family during the Holocaust, Frankl was sent to Auschwitz, the worst of all the concentration camps. In his memoir he discusses the life lessons he learned while everything was stripped from him. He was forced to walk in the snow with minimal clothing, beaten on a regular basis, malnourished, and mentally abused. One of the most profound lessons Victor Frankl shares with us is possibly one of the most important lessons we can grasp in life.

> We who lived in concentration camps can remember the men who walked through the huts comforting others, giving away their last piece of bread. They may have been few in number, but they offer sufficient **proof that everything can be taken from a man but one thing: the last of the human freedoms — to choose one's attitude in any given set of circumstances, to choose one's own way.**

We certainly don't have to endure the degrees of pain and suffering that Viktor Frankl endured, but times are tough for the millennial generation, considering how affluent so many Americans are in general. I know I don't have to tell the current senior who's trying to find a job right now, because they are seeing these difficulties first-hand. The economy is still slow as a result of the 2008 crisis. The world we live in is becoming more and more competitive as we continue to become more of a global economy. College debt is continuing to climb to new highs. There are over one trillion dollars of student loans outstanding. Just yesterday (as I write this) the Dow Jones Industrial dropped 318 points, the largest loss in over a year. Almost 50 percent of college graduates are unemployed or underemployed. With an average student carrying about $25,000 in student debt and grim prospects for full employment, students are reverting to bartending and waiting on tables. Too many students are pondering why they even went to college in the first place.

You're not just competing with the forty or one hundred kids in class with you, or the more than 15 million students enrolled in college now in the United States. You're also competing with young people from India, China, Brazil, and other countries. You are competing against students who've chosen to get a master's degree because they couldn't get a job a few years back. They're now well-equipped with a higher degree, as they compete for the same jobs as undergraduates. I'm not trying to scare you; this is simply the market environment we're living in today. How do we combat such headwinds? The answer is: unrelenting persistence. When the going gets tough, the tough get going. Students are doing that now.

A good friend of mine just locked down an offer for graduate school – free tuition, and all expenses paid. I just received other news about a student who, just two weeks after we discussed strategies together, has an internship working in the exact area of public relations he wanted, in which he'll make $2,000 for the semester (for 15 hours a week).

The changing environment requires an increase in pro-activeness and effort. You've made the first big step as you're reading this book. I want to help make you ready, with the mindset to be successful in *any* economic climate or circumstance.

The first step in maximizing your effort levels is to surround yourself with the best people, because whether you've thought about it or not, you're a combination of the five people you spend the most time with on a daily basis. This is very powerful and should not be overlooked.

A few months back I mentored a college freshman named Lauren. We strategized how she'd go about getting the internship she wanted, which could put her in a great position to get an associate media position upon graduation. She came to me doubting that it would be possible, because her "friends" had laughed when she brought the idea to them. After we talked again, she set a goal of reading one book on social media marketing or production media every week. When Thursday arrived, the big night to go out to the bars downtown, I came out of my fraternity meeting and saw Lauren, upset. Her friends had called her several times to go out, and they'd been sending her mean messages about missing the evening with them. After talking about it, she came to the conclusion that they weren't true friends if they weren't interested in seeing her reach her full potential. Lauren slowly disengaged from that group of friends, and now feels several pounds lighter. Lauren is doing great and is well on her way to getting that associate's role.

You've got to really apply yourself. Cut out the lazy naps (although you should still nap if you pulled an all-nighter to write a paper!) and make it a goal to get up by a certain time. If you set big enough goals (per chapter two), you'll need the time in the morning to start making your way through them. Get out of bed with a make-things-happen mentality. Write your goals down on a legal pad and let that focus you on your schedule for the day.

Don't EVER make excuses. At my house we used to have a saying that went, "Excuses are like butt holes, everyone has them and they all stink." We each have the ability to choose our own way in any given set of circumstances, to make decisions for ourselves. With that said, what we choose to do or not do boils down to a matter of priorities. To *not* get something done means it wasn't enough of a priority. Do yourself a big favor: try not to let yourself off the hook.

Adopt a no-skip policy when it comes to classes. In the famous words of Woody Allen, "Ninety percent of success is just showing up." You never know what you might miss if you choose to skip class. The guest speaker who might be the gateway to your first internship could be there, and one simple hit of the snooze button could cost you dearly. Be the person who always shows up – that's something to be proud of, and people admire it.

Meet the following minimum quota to get the internship or job you want in one month:

1. Make at least 20 cold calls a day, following the advice discussed earlier.
2. Send a minimum of 50 cold emails every day.
3. Ask two current contacts each day if they know anyone who might be able to help you. It's totally acceptable to reach out to family. I actually highly encourage you to talk with uncles, aunts, or cousins, which I'll bet is something you haven't done yet. What are you waiting for? They're already in your corner – that's a great place to start.
4. Read 20 pages a day of an industry publication of your choice. I particularly like the *Economist*, the *Wall Street Journal*, *New York Times*, *Deal Book*, *Financial Times*, and *Fortune* magazine.

5. Then read 30 pages of a book that will help you learn more about the industry or field you're prospecting.

6. If there are any interview guides for your target industry, make sure to get one section done a day (20 pages if the sections are overly long).

This may seem intense, but it really only takes a maximum of four hours a day. You owe it to yourself, your family, and those close to you. I highly recommend you read Grant Cardone's 10X rule for more details. Don't wait for it to come to you — go out and get it. As the football coach at my high school always used to say, "Every day is a great day to get better." The days we have here are limited. So make sure to make each day count.

Abraham Lincoln best embodies the concepts I'm trying to communicate in this chapter. Below is a simple timeline of his life:

Age 9: his mother died.

Age 22: he lost his job because the company he worked for went bankrupt.

Age 23: Lincoln ran for state legislature and came in eighth out of thirteen candidates.

Age 24: he borrowed money to start a business. The business failed before the first fiscal year closed. The local government seized his possessions to pay off his debt. His partner died, leaving Lincoln with his partner's debt as well. He spent several years paying off all the debt.

Age 25: he ran for state legislature again and finally won.

Age 26: he was engaged to a beautiful young woman, who died before the wedding could take place.

Age 27: Lincoln plunged into a depression and suffered a nervous breakdown.

Age 29: he wanted to become the speaker of the state legislature. He was defeated in a landslide.

Age 34: he campaigned for a U.S. congressional seat and lost.

Age 35: he ran for Congress again. This time he won.

Age 39: when his term ended, he was unemployed due to the single-term limit.

Age 40: he applied to be the commissioner of the General Land Office, but was rejected.

Age 45: he campaigned for the U.S. Senate and lost by six electoral votes.

Age 47: he was one of the contenders for the vice-presidential nomination at his party's national convention. He lost.

Age 49: he ran for the U.S. Senate seat a second time. And for the second time, he lost.

Age 51: after a life full of failing, disappointing, losing loved ones, and setbacks, Abraham Lincoln was elected the sixteenth president of the United States.

Lessons

1. Surround yourself with the best people you can.
2. Push yourself.
3. Think big.
4. "Every day is a great day to get better."
5. When you want to quit, think of Honest Abe. Persevere.

CHAPTER 13

Steps to the Top - The 10 Laws of Intern Success

"Things turn out best for the people who
make the best of the way things turn out."
—John Wooden

"Good, better, best. Never let it rest. Until your
good is better and your better is best."
—Tim Duncan

The Ten Laws

1. Have a good attitude. No one likes to work with
    someone who's irritable or outright uninterested.

It's amazing how much difference just having a good attitude will make. Having a good attitude means being excited to be a part of the organization, greeting people as you see them around the office, and never acting disgruntled about any task given to you. At the end of the day, you are an intern. Although most employers try their hardest to give you tasks that will be beneficial for you, most internships will involve some work that isn't the most scintillating. If you are incapable of taking these assignments on and producing good work, there's a high chance that you will not get the more interesting work when it comes in.

2. Be the first one in the office in the morning and the last one to leave. You are interning for someone who has taken a chance on you and believed in you enough to hire you. Don't forget that it's a privilege to be there. Take advantage of the opportunity and make every minute count. If you leave at five p.m., when you could have stayed until six p.m., you may have let an hour of learning slip away. There are some people who are more intelligent than yourself working there, so take advantage of having access to them.

3. Don't be a robot. If the person you're working for gives you an assignment, don't do just the

bare minimum. Try to add more value or take the assignment the extra step in any way possible.

4. Go the extra mile without being asked. If you have down time, don't waste it. Learn what tasks add value to the person you're working for and spend your "free" time trying to make a work product that will help them in some way. This is hard to do in the first couple weeks, but you'll get better at it once you get into the rhythm of things. Don't be surprised by how many people take notice of your efforts.

5. Ask good questions. There's a fine line between the right amount of questions and too many. Always exhaust any and all resources at your disposal before approaching the person above you. The higher-up's time is very valuable and they don't want to be spending a lot of time helping you with something that you could have found the answer to in a five-second Google search. Be resourceful.

6. Carry a notebook with you at all times. Write everything down. Anytime you hear a term or acronym that you don't understand, write it down and look it up later. Keep a list of your questions, so that you can Google the questions later. If you can't find the answers, make sure to take the entire list of questions that you have compiled over time so that

you aren't just bringing one question at a time to your superior. People are much more appreciative of an intern coming and asking several questions at once, rather than coming in every couple of minutes to ask one question at a time.

7. Own your work. When you start with a new firm, everything you do helps develop your brand. You want to establish yourself as the person who does great work. One of the ways to do this is by making sure you read voraciously and do as much as you can to learn about the business before starting. And make sure you always print your work and check it before you send it to a superior – for some reason it's much easier to catch errors on paper rather than on a screen. Have you ever wondered why two students doing the same internship with the same interests come out with a different view of the experience? If you establish yourself as the person who produces error-free work on time or early, then you'll be given the most interesting work that comes in the door. If you make too many mistakes in the beginning, you'll very likely get put on the mundane tasks that aren't nearly as exciting.

8. Don't assume the internship will teach you anything. As much as possible, try to teach yourself the work and skill set prior to joining. It will give you a leg

up on other interns, while at the same time giving you the opportunity to take on more challenging projects that may come your way.

9. If you're given flexibility to work on your own projects, do so carefully. Try to find something that you are knowledgeable about, something that the company lacks. Look to see if the company is expanding into a new market or is trying new technology. If they are, become the expert in that area or technology. That means reading everything on the subject, *and* any other related material available to you. If the company doesn't have any testimonials or isn't experienced with video, this can be your area to add value. Many students are able to bring value through social media. If you tackle that, make sure you're using social media for the purpose of increasing exposure and sales. This will dramatically increase your chances of securing a full-time offer when you finish the internship. (Remember the saying, "Follow the money"?)

10. Be thankful. This is brief because later there's a whole chapter on this subject.

CHAPTER 14

Ibuprofen of Business

"Criticism may not be agreeable, but it is necessary.
It fulfills the same function as pain in the human body.
It calls attention to an unhealthy state of things."
—Winston Churchill

"I like criticism. It makes you strong."
—LeBron James

You have now been in your internship or job for a few weeks or months. You've been busting your tail to make a positive impression, learn as much as you can, and add value to the people you're interning under. You have been trying many different strategies to increase your efficiency or make fewer mistakes. You think everything's going well, but you haven't had the opportunity to get much feedback. How do you know you're doing well?

While interviewing people for this book, I came across a junior at a state school who'd been interning for a marketing firm for about a month.

"I wasn't assigned anything too difficult. I was getting my work done early and I thought the work was great. After completing a project, the person I was interning for fired me. All she said was that it wasn't working out. My internship ended with that."

Take a lesson from that: constructive criticism should be your best friend. It's the best mechanism we have to gain feedback. Without feedback, we lack sufficient tools to understand how we're doing. If we're unable to benchmark our performance against ourselves and others, we lack the information necessary to improve. An intern not checking in for feedback is like LeBron James not obtaining a record for his wins and losses. Without LeBron knowing whether he's winning or losing games, how would he determine which of his strategies are most beneficial or least beneficial? Athletes are generally fortunate to have fairly frequent feedback loops that allow them to make adjustments to improve. In the NFL, you have a game every week (except your team's buy week). You practice and prepare for your opponent and receive feedback on your strengths and weaknesses throughout the game.

Or better yet, think of a boxer. After every round the boxers go to their corners to discuss what is working and is not working. Angelo Dundee was the corner man and coach for Muhammad Ali, George Foreman, and Sugar Ray Leonard. Here's Sugar Ray Leonard sitting down with National Public Radio for an interview to talk about his coach.

> National Public Radio Host: I am curious to know what he said to you in 1979. This is after you won your biggest match to date at that point. It was a NBC welterweight fight. You beat Wilfred Benitez. And it — obviously, it was a grueling match, down to almost the bitter end. It was called in your favor with just six seconds on the clock. What did Dundee say to you after you got the title? Sugar Ray Leonard: That fight took so much out of me because I never stopped throwing punches. I tried to throw as many as possible. And Angelo just said after the fight: "Great job." And that solidified that I won the fight.

Notice that it wasn't even the act of winning the fight that confirmed the victory for Sugar Ray Leonard. It was his coach's feedback that affirmed the monumental win.

As interns, employees, entrepreneurs, sons, daughter, or students – we all need access to feedback. The trick is knowing how to manage gaining the feedback. I think we're all comfortable with the fact that knowledge about how we're doing in different facets of life is generally helpful, but we aren't entirely sure about how to have those conversations. Try commenting to an acquaintance, "You are really impatient, you should try learning the virtue of patience in life." We all know that would be an effective way to become disliked by many. It's amazing how we all desire approval on a certain level, but we dread anyone condemning us.

We're taught to view constructive criticism in a negative light, with harsh implications. This should not be the case. Good constructive feedback can result in such positive changes in our life. Feedback from those closest to us is how we grow as people. It allows us to get a better handle on our strengths and expand upon them. It also allows us to hear our shortcomings, so that we can improve our weaknesses. What if the student we were just talking about needed to change the presentation of his work slightly to make the internship work? It sure would have helped his situation to get feedback before it escalated to the point where he was let go.

I recommend starting small. List the five people who are closest to you. This could be your mom, dad, brother, sister, grandparents, aunt, uncle, best friend, or significant other. Send them an email or text message asking them if they'd be willing to take a few minutes over the next week to answer two questions for you. The first would be, "What do you feel are my three biggest strengths?" Second, "What do you think are my three largest weaknesses?" The answer to these two questions will allow you to immediately start improving yourself by maximizing your strengths and shoring up your weaknesses.

Let's assume you employ the strategies and tactics laid out in earlier chapters, and you're now in the internship opportunity you imagined. You're working for one of the best players in your particular industry, and you want to know how everything is going.

How do I bring up the conversation?

Timing is critical. No one appreciates the intern who comes up to their superior after two days on the job, asking for feedback. At the same time you don't want to wait too long, and not have enough time to improve after receiving feedback. Since most internships are about two to three months long, we'll assume that timeframe. I recommend you introduce yourself to the people you'll work closely with, and try to have lunch with them in the first two weeks. After about three weeks, reach out for feedback. The goal of this email I've reproduced here is to thank your employer again for the opportunity, remind them of the projects you've been working on, and ask for a few minutes of their time to get constructive criticism. I would recommend sending the following email. It will work perfectly for what you're trying to accomplish.

> Dear (Insert Superior's name),
>
> I have really enjoyed my first few weeks interning under you, and I wanted to thank you again for the opportunity. (insert the projects you have been working on) have been a great learning experience. I was wondering if I could get a few minutes of your time this week to get feedback on what I am doing well and things I could improve upon. I am available during the following times:
>
> Tuesday, June 10, from 8 to 11:30 AM
> Wednesday, June 11, from 3 to 6:30 PM
>
> If neither of those times work for you, we can find another time to talk. I'm looking forward to speaking with you.
>
> Sincerely,
> John Smith

There are some points to remember when you send the email above. Include specific projects that you worked on with this person to help jog their memory, and to allow them to prepare better feedback and criticism. Make sure you list all the possible times you're available to meet. Including potential times eliminates the unnecessary email exchange of trying to figure something out. This is quite helpful to busy superiors.

What are the best strategies for getting honest constructive criticism?

One of the worst things you can do when you're receiving negative feedback is to get defensive or visibly upset. If you show you're upset, your superior may feel forced to sugarcoat the rest of their message, weakening the feedback and rendering it much less valuable. Of course, this is easier said than done. Mark Twain once said, "There are two types of speakers. Those that get nervous talking in front of others, and those that are lying." The same holds true for receiving constructive criticism. No one really enjoys hearing about their shortcomings. However, there are some tactics that can help you receive the feedback with more grace, thereby maximizing the benefits.

If you can, it's optimal to view the person delivering the feedback in a positive light. See them as the coach who wants you to succeed and reach your goals. Going into the discussion thinking that they have negative intentions is a recipe for disaster. Also, view the criticism you receive through this lens: the feedback offers you an opportunity to improve. From a career standpoint, it's a guide for bettering yourself. Very few high achievers in this world, if any, had a record of all wins and top achievements. Do you think Abraham Lincoln would have been the sixteenth president of the United States if he'd viewed each failure as a *failure*? Probably not. He was able to learn something from each experience and leverage that learning to become a better politician, leader, and communicator.

Let the other person carry the conversation. The goal of the feedback session is to learn as much as you can about your strengths, weaknesses, and opportunities. We do very little learning when our mouths are running. By being receptive and taking notes, you allow your supervisor to give the honest feedback you need.

Try to have this conversation in private. Having others around would really put a damper on the openness required to make the meeting successful. Private offices, conference rooms, or secluded restaurant tables are the best settings.

Finally, if you can admit fault, do so. While admitting fault, you open yourself up. You become vulnerable. When someone is vulnerable, others around you become much more likely to open up themselves. How many times have you had a conversation with someone in which you shared information about yourself that was deeper than small talk? Any comment that sparked some adrenaline in you and made you a little nervous, would in turn mean that you'd be greeted with a similarly meaningful comment from the other person, and the next thing you know, the connection was much deeper than before. Do anything you can do to make the other person more comfortable.

What questions are best to ask?

Most of the time your supervisor will take control of the conversation. They might offer some small talk about your experience thus far, and then dive into their assessment of what you're doing right and what can be improved. On the other hand, if they *don't* take charge of the conversation, your discussion can be as simple as you would like it to be. For example, you could use the following script to start things off.

"Thank you so much for taking the time to meet with me. I have had a great experience thus far working on (insert your projects). I really admire what you've been able to accomplish thus far in your career and wanted to get some feedback from you on how I am doing. Maybe talk through some things that I can improve on, and review the things I'm doing well on?"

That should kick off the conversation. From there, be all ears.

How long should I give between feedback loops?

I recommend waiting about a month in between feedback loops for an internship. If it's a full-time job, then I suggest meeting to get feedback quarterly (every three months). Of course this will vary from organization to organization, but the people I surveyed agreed on that recommended time frame.

Once I get the feedback, how do I implement it?

This is the exciting part: the opportunity to implement the advice you've just received. In order to fully comprehend and review the feedback, you have to take detailed notes. If you don't want to take notes during the conversation, be sure to document as much as you can afterwards. Once you have a written record of what you're doing well and how you can improve, it's time to execute. Here are my most helpful tips to executing on the advice:

1. Make improvement part of your daily goals, which you'll write down and review every morning and night.
2. Set reminders for two times a day on Microsoft Outlook. Type in your top three strengths and ask yourself: am I still doing these things? Below that, type in the top three improvements, and ask: what am I doing to improve these? If you're are on the move a lot with your internship or job, put the reminders in your phone – the first, an hour after you get into the office every day, and the second, right after you get back from lunch.

3. If you like more physical reminders, you can place post-it notes on your monitor. If you spend a lot of time in the office, this will be effective.

4. Share the top points from the conversation with trusted peers and ask them to check in with you on how you're doing.

Basically, we have two mechanisms to track progress in every aspect of our lives. The first is through our own judgments. Unfortunately, we are often very lenient with ourselves when we are succeeding, and very tough on ourselves during tough times. Although self-reflection is encouraged and extremely beneficial, it's helpful to gain outside perspectives through constructive criticism. Constructive criticism removes our personal bias and allows us to see different perspectives.

CHAPTER 15

Personal Board of Directors

"Tell me and I forget, teach me and I may
remember, involve me and I learn."
—Benjamin Franklin

"I think a role model is a mentor - someone you
see on a daily basis, and you learn from them."
—Denzel Washington

There is no doubt that I wouldn't be in the position I am
today if it weren't for the incredible men and women who
have taken the time to mentor me throughout my journey
thus far. Professional athletes know this sentiment to be

true, as they train with the best teachers and coaches in their respective sports. Corporations have boards of directors that are usually composed of experienced and knowledgeable people who provide guidance to the company's senior leadership. Most famous musicians had apprenticeships under more senior musicians who were world-class in their genres. More and more organizations are adopting mentor programs every day. Why? Because they work. I am a very big believer in being a self-starter, and that with persistence and determination you can accomplish anything. But it's much harder to do that on your own. If you take the time to study any of the top performers in your field of interest, chances are you'll find that they had a role model, someone who shared their skill and experience with them, a person who gave them guidance along the way. Very few people, if any, journey to the top of their field on their own. Aspiring medical students learn under older, more experienced doctors. An artist's painting techniques are not developed until they are able to learn under the wing of a more skilled master of their trade. As another example, let's take a quick glimpse into the life of Warren Buffett. He is commonly considered the most successful investor of the twentieth century (and he's still going strong). Mr. Buffett was the world's wealthiest person in 2008, and he is one of history's most generous philanthropists. Did Mr. Buffett pave the way for his own success without a mentor? No. Warren Buffett encountered a professor that he really admired early in his career. Benjamin Graham was that professor, friend, mentor, and father figure for Buffett.

Warren Buffett sought wisdom and advice from Benjamin Graham, his former professor at Columbia University. Graham was so important that Buffett's biographer devoted an entire chapter to him in *Buffett: The Making of An American Capitalist*, including this: "Ben Graham opened the door in a way that spoke to Buffett personally. He gave Buffett the tools to explore the market's manifold possibilities, and also an approach that fit his student's temper."

Graham was much more than Buffett's professor. It was Graham who provided Buffett with the lens through which Buffett would view investing. Buffett absolutely aspired to follow in Graham's footsteps, religiously reading Graham's publications such as "The Intelligent Investor" and "Securities Analysis." Upon hearing of Graham's appointment as chairman of GEICO, Buffett made a trip to Washington – if Graham was the chairman of GEICO, Buffett had to learn more about the company. He asked questions of employees to gather more information about the company. Buffett looked up to Graham as his hero. Little did he know the destiny that would lie ahead of him in the years to follow.

Denzel Washington also had a mentor early on. He remembers Billy Thomas as being an important person to his ten-year-old self. The director of the Boys and Girls Club, Mr. Thomas made a point to display the school pennants of the kids who went to college. Denzel remembers looking up at those pennants and thinking, "If I work hard, I can go to college, anything is possible." He remembers Billy Thomas telling him he could do anything he wanted to do. It seems like a simple message, but it certainly had a profound impact on the two-time Oscar winner. He doesn't recall hearing the message of opportunity too much at home. It was his time with his mentor that allowed him to change the trajectory of his life.

The process of learning from and asking questions of those more experienced than we are has always been one of the most successful systems for exchanging ideas, innovation, future development, and overall advancement. As Warren Buffett, Denzel Washington, and so many others have utilized the power of mentors, so can we.

How to find a mentor

Not just any person can be your mentor. It takes a special person with enough confidence to give back, and the humility to acknowledge that someone else did the same for them. The ideal mentor is someone whose footsteps you'd like to follow in the future. If you admire not only their career success, but how they manage the rest of their life as well, that's ideal. The best mentors for me have been simply amazing people. A mentor from my college years has pretty much become a second dad to me, and I have not necessarily been able to add any value to him in return. If you can find a person who loves to teach and give back, you've hit the jackpot. Cherish that relationship, because they aren't that common. Ignore anyone who says that a mentor has to be a certain age. One of my mentors who really helped me though the investment banking process was only twenty-seven. So don't put constraints on age. If you respect someone and feel that their guidance would be beneficial, go for it.

How do I start the process of a mentor relationship?

Having someone become a mentor is not a really formal process. The best mentor relationships come about in two main ways. The first is through reaching out for inspiring dialogue. If that meeting goes well, ask if you can keep in touch if you have the occasional question moving forward. A "yes" here gives you the green light to stay in touch. I highly recommend that you send them any relevant news or information that might be helpful to them as a way to keep the contact going — anytime that you can create a good reason to reach out and connect, do it. Make it a habit. Every time you correspond or meet in person, the relationship deepens. Over time, if the person feels that being a mentor is appropriate, they will take on that role for you.

Don☺t be impatient

I see too many college students meet someone they really like and ask them to be their mentor right off the bat. This rarely works out for the best. Most senior professionals are alarmed by this, because they hardly know you after one meeting, yet after one meeting you're already asking for a large commitment from them. You need to show interest in them first and have the patience to allow the relationship to develop. There are many interests you might have in common that can help to strengthen the bond over time, such as when you mutually:

- Support the same sports team
- Enjoy traveling
- Have a similar artistic taste
- Enjoy skiing, fishing, golfing, hunting, etc.
- Read similar books or blogs
- Grew up in the same city
- Had a similar upbringing
- Play the same sports
- Eat at the same favorite restaurants
- Collect the same items
- Embarked on a similar career path
- Attended the same university or high school

I could go on and on about having things you may have in common, any of which provide the opportunity for you to get to know each other outside of work or the professional arena.

How can you benefit your mentor?

That's a good question. A few of my best mentors who are on my board of directors have never necessarily received any value from me. I haven't interned for them, or solved any of their business issues. Despite that, these people have given me so much of their time, and they've helped me in ways that I never thought possible. Time and time again I've heard from very successful people about their inflection point; when someone took the time to mentor them. Most people can recall that one person who really took a chance on them, the person who took them under their wing when they were no one. Just as that mentor did for them, a lot of people would like to pay it forward to another young person.

It is an opportunity for them to give back, and maybe that's all the benefit that your mentor needs. The best value you can provide to them is to listen and apply the ideas they provide for you. This relationship works best when your success is their success as well. Most importantly, always be grateful. It takes times and energy to be a mentor.

The best uses for a mentor?

I have formed a board of Ten mentors whom I consult on every important career decision. When I was considering the offers I had on the table after my internship with Goldman Sachs, I reached out to this group for their guidance. When I first became interested in finance, I reached out to the few mentors I had, asking what I needed to do to get to where I wanted to go. Mentors provide career advice, knowledge, and experience. They can provide insight that will help you perform in internships and interviews. Mentors have networks that tend to be fairly large, so they can also provide great connections to people that you might not have access to, after having been in the workplace for (perhaps) many years, attending conferences, and perhaps working at several different firms. I also really enjoy getting together with my mentors. Whether playing golf, getting lunch at our favorite restaurants, talking about our sports teams, or getting updates on neat trips they are taking, I really value the time I get to spend with them, and I make sure to remind them of the impact they've had on my life.

CHAPTER 16

Thank You

"The joy I get from winning a major championship
doesn't even compare to the feeling I get
when a kid writes a letter saying: 'Thank you
so much. You have changed my life.'"
—Tiger Woods

"For all the supporters of Tesla over the years,
and it's been several years now and there have
been some very tough times, I'd just like to say
thank you very much. I deeply appreciate the
support, particularly through the darkest times."
—Elon Musk

As a society, we generally accept that a sense of gratitude
is a good quality in a person. After all, gratitude is one of

the original virtues in Aristotle's ethics framework. Who doesn't enjoy a thank you in return for their good deed or action? Yet while we may hold gratitude in high regard, we are not all in the habit of saying thank you. I've seen this over and over in the millennial generation cohort. Let us take a deeper dive into the effects of saying thank you.

Professor Grant of Wharton and Professor Gino of Harvard performed a study looking at the effects of gratitude. They asked fifty-seven students to give feedback on a student cover letter. Half of the students received an email simply confirming that their feedback was received. The other half received a message of thank you and appreciation. Only 25 percent of the people in the first group felt an increase in self-worth, but 55 percent of the group that received thanks received a boost in self-worth. To take the study even further, students in each group were asked if they could do that same thing for another study seeking feedback. Only 32 percent of the first group was willing to help the second student. More than double (66 percent) of the second group that received thanks the first time around were willing to help.

Although this study was done on students, the same holds true for any human being. We all like to feel appreciated and we expect to be thanked for our efforts. This includes all the people who take the time to mentor you, sit down to meet for coffee, or extend you an internship. So how can we adopt the power of thank you into the concepts laid out in this book?

Make it a habit now. Always thank people for what they do for you. When I was a kid, I had a sleepover at a friend's house. My dad came to pick me up in the morning and as we were driving away, he asked if I'd said thank you. I hadn't – I'd completely forgotten. Dad turned the car around and made me go up to my hosts' door to say thank you. In that moment of embarrassment, I decided to make sure I wouldn't ever do that again. Saying thank you to others is the least you can do.

After an internship, hand write thank you notes to the people who took the time to teach you something. They are all busy, and they could have used that time to do something for themselves, but they didn't. They chose to invest time in you.

I try to make an effort to reach out and thank the people who have helped me over the past few years. I actually just paused in writing this chapter to thank a few of the people on my personal board of directors. One thing to keep in mind is that you can never really thank someone too much. When you are unsure, remember this:

For this book, I had the opportunity to interview a very senior level human resources professional who has worked with two Fortune 100 companies. Initially, I reached out to her for commentary on the importance of internships. The conversation shifted when we started talking about two interns that she'd had in the office the previous semester. One was from a very prestigious school, had a 3.98 GPA, did very good work, and got along just fine with the people in his group. The HR person I was interviewing, an alumna of the same school, had played a large role in helping him get the role. The second intern was from a much smaller school, didn't have near the GPA of the first intern, and his work product was just not that great. The company actually let him go a week early to avoid that having to pay him the final week. The group supervisor was fine with that, as she didn't feel the second intern was adding to much value to the group. The HR person I was interviewing really liked that second intern, though. He was always thankful of everything anyone did for him, and was just generally more appreciative of the opportunity. I thought this was interesting and wanted to learn more. I asked the HR person, "You said 'more appreciative,' – was the first intern not grateful for the opportunity?" It turned out that the first intern had the attitude that the internship was a given. Students from his school regularly interned there and they took it for granted. He never thanked anyone for the opportunity or even thanked anyone in his group. Out of curiosity I asked, "Who would you refer to another person if asked which intern they should take?" She paused, "I can't believe I am going to say this, but the second one. He was just much easier to relate to."

That is the power of gratitude. Although the second intern wasn't the best in terms of performance, he would get recommended because he showed appreciation. Gratitude played a significant role in his being "easier to relate to."

The opportunity to give back and pay it forward was my biggest motivation for writing this book. All I ask of you is when you reach a point in your career where you have an opportunity to mentor a younger professional or take on an intern, do that. We don't go about the journey alone. Just as people will help you get internships and teach you, so should you do the same for the next generation.

Lessons

1. Be thankful.
2. Make thanking people a habit.
3. Send thank you notes or thank you emails to the people who give you their time.
4. Thank the people responsible for giving you an internship opportunity.
5. Remember that what goes around comes around.

Works Cited

Arora, Swati. "Famous Mentors and Their Famous
    Mentees." Mentorpolis. N.p., 15 Oct. 2012. Web. 26
    Feb. 2014.

Cardone, Grant. The 10x Rule: The Only Difference
    between Success and Failure. Hoboken, NJ: John
    Wiley & Sons, 2011. Print.

Carpenter, Julia. "Five Internship Secrets from
    Superstar College Interns." CNN. Cable News
    Network, 01 Jan. 1970. Web. 26 Feb. 2014.

Cohn, Gary. "Media Relations." Gary Cohn, Kogod
    School of Business Speaker. American University,
    10 May 2009. Web. 26 Feb. 2014.

Dr. Matthews, Gail. "Study Backs up Strategies
    for Achieving Goals." Dominican University of
    California. N.p., n.d. Web. 25 Feb. 2014.

Dundee, Angelo, Guy Raz, and Sugar Ray Leonard.
    "Angelo Dundee, More Than Just a Good
    Cornerman." NPR. NPR, 04 Feb. 2012. Web.
    26 Feb. 2014.

Ferrazzi, Keith, and Tahl Raz. Never Eat Alone. New York: Doubleday, 2009. Print.

Glickman, Jodi. "HBR Blog Network." Harvard Business Review. N.p., 06 July 2011. Web. 26 Feb. 2014.

Hering, Beth Braccio. "Why Are Internships So Important?" CNN. Cable News Network, 14 Apr. 2010. Web. 26 Feb. 2014.

Kingkade, Tyler. "Tips for Internships: 13 Bits Of Advice To Make Your Summer Awesome." The Huffington Post. TheHuffingtonPost.com, 18 June 2012. Web. 26 Feb. 2014.

Korn, Melissa. "The Importance of Being an Intern." Wall Street Journal. N.p., 18 June 2013. Web. 26 Feb. 2014.

Leddy, Chuck. "The Power of 'thanks' | Harvard Gazette." Harvard Gazette. Harvard University, 19 Mar. 2013. Web. 18 Mar. 2014.

Lipson, Debra. "17 Incredible Successful People Who Started As Interns." The Huffington Post. TheHuffingtonPost.com, 03 Oct. 2013. Web. 26 Feb. 2014.

Lowenstein, Roger. Buffett: The Making of an American Capitalist. New York: Random House, 1995. Print.

Luzer, Daniel. "The Student Loan Debt Problem:
    Focus on Public Colleges." The Huffington Post.
    TheHuffingtonPost.com, 29 Aug. 2013. Web. 26
    Feb. 2014.

"Recruiting Benchmarks: Offers and
    Acceptances." Recruiting Benchmarks: Offers and
    Acceptances. National Association of Colleges and
    Employers, n.d. Web. 01 Feb. 2014.

Wargo, Eric. "How Many Seconds to a First
    Impression?" Association for Psychological Science
    RSS. N.p., n.d. Web. 05 Sept. 2013.

Washington, Denzel. "Mentor Gave Me Confidence to
    Succeed." CNN. Cable News Network, 30 Sept.
    2010. Web. 26 Feb. 2014.

White, Martha C. "Business & Money." Business Money
    The Real Reason New College Grads Cant Get
    Hired Comments. Times, n.d. Web. 25 Feb. 2014.

Thank you to my family, friends, mentors, and teachers. A special thank you to my incredible parents. I can't thank them enough for all the support they have given me over the years.

Thank you to the people that helped make this happen :

Amanda Larocco

Beth Hair

Capozzoli Family

Caitlin Shaughnessy

Foster Family

Gray Nester

Jay McBride

Mike Foy

Molly Stanley

Shaughnessy Family

Staci McBride

Stuart Hair

Tim Burson

Wallace Family

CPSIA information can be obtained at www.ICGtesting.com
Printed in the USA
LVOW02s0915110115

422341LV00028B/1035/P